For R B.
Thank yr
interest in a
"God Bless"

Gene Browning
Mueber Browning

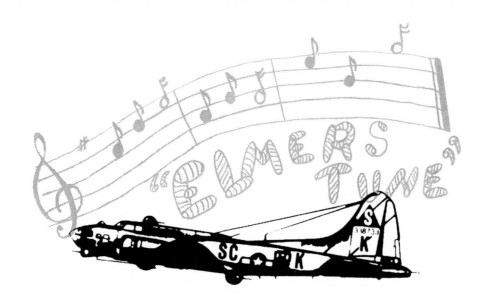

ELMER'S TUNE

by Elmer Eugene Browning

Ball Turret Gunner B-17

and Melba Archer Browning

Peppertree Press

Sarasota, Florida

For information regarding permission,
call 941-922-2662 or contact us at our website:
www.peppertreepublishing.com or write to:
the Peppertree Press, LLC.
Attention: Publisher
1269 First Street, Suite 7
Sarasota, Florida 34236

ISBN: 978-0-9817572-1-6

Library of Congress Number: 2008928627

Printed in the U.S.A.

Printed June 2008

This book is dedicated to:

ALL THE MEN WHO GAVE THEIR LIVES FOR AMERICA AND
THEIR WOMEN WHO LOST THE LOVE OF THEIR LIFE AND
THE CHILDREN THAT LOST THEIR FATHERS AND MOTHERS

And Especially to:

THE BEST PILOT IN THE E.T.O.
LT. ELMER C. GILLESPIE
AND HIS CREW

LT. THEODORE CHAPMAN
CO-PILOT

LT. HODGE E. MASON
NAVIGATOR

LT. DAVID L. TAYLOR
BOMBARDIER

DON D. ZIRBEL - T/SGT.
ENGINEER

CHARLES A. MC FALL
T/SGT. RADIO OPERATOR

JEFFERSON D. DICKSON
S/SGT. TAILGUNNER

ROBERT J. BUSH
S/SGT. RIGHT WAIST GUNNER

THOMAS M. LAMBERT
S/SGT. LEFT WAIST GUNNER

ELMER E. BROWNING - S/SGT.
S/SGT. BALL TURRET GUNNER

This is a story about
The roaring sound of the B-17
And it's beauty that still holds me spellbound.

———————————————————

When I stand beside her and go back in time, I can still
Feel the presence of my old crew and the cold chills
Running down my spine.
For those of us who flew the missions, she will always be

THE STAR

Always, a big shinning FORTRESS

MAY GOD BLESS AMERICA
THE LAND THAT I LOVE

CONTRAILS IN THE SKY

I saw those contrails blossom in the foggy England sky.
I heard the hymn of airmen who were too young to die.
I did not see them dying; I could not feel their pain.
I only knew they loved us, and their love was not in vain.
I saw the planes assemble in Europe's cloudy sky
I saw them drop their bomb loads, and I knew that some would die.
I did not know their names then; I knew not the reason why.
I only knew the turmoil when man takes to the sky.
I saw those wing tips glisten in England long ago.
I heard the roar of engines that strained to meet the foe.
I did not know the purpose; I did not know the plan.
I only knew that this was war, and it was made by man.
It is for us, the living, to work with faith and trust,
To stop this bloody fighting or sink into the dust.
If we would shirk our duties, let ignorance be unfurled,
We'll see those contrails blossom in the skies around the world.

—Austin L. Alsop

POSITION UPON ENTERING THE TURRET
FROM THE INSIDE OF THE PLANE

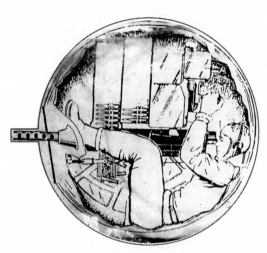

POSITION AFTER TURNING ON
THE POWER AND ROLLING BACK
INTO THE FIRING POSITION

Preface

The first time I got into the ball turret when we were in flight, I turned on the power switch, and pulled the control handle back into a firing position. I felt as if the turret had come loose from the plane, and I was tumbling toward the earth. I climbed back out into the plane and said, "I'm not riding in that"! Then I looked down at it, and it had not come loose from the plane. It was harder to get back down into it the second time, but I knew all the other jobs were also hard for the rest of the crew. This happened when we first started training as a crew of ten in an actual B-17 in Dyersburg, Tennessee. Prior to that, the ball turret was attached to something other than a plane for training purposes. It was fun, at that time, for the simulation of planes coming toward you, and shooting was like a game, but once, the ball turret was attached to a moving B-17, the motion of the plane made it a very scary place to be. I was proud and scared but I was part of a crew, and I knew that I could count on the others, and that they were depending on me.

The photos above shows the position of the person inside the ball turret, and when I first stepped down into the ball turret, I had to lean all the way forward for the hatch to be closed, and when I turned on the power switches, it rolled the ball turret down to where I was in the fetal position.

When the guns were in the firing position, the hatch was completely outside the plane. There was no room for a parachute inside the ball turret, so it was kept in the plane just outside the ball turret, and I wore the harness to hook to it should I need it in a hurry.

THE CREW OF ELMER'S TUNE

I have called this story: Elmer's Tune, because of our pilot: ELMER GILLESPIE, a wonderful pilot that brought his crew of ten men all home safely after 35 missions to the most wonderful place in the world: HOME, LOCATED IN THE UNITED STATES OF AMERICA.

This is written in the first person, because it is a series of events that happened over the years during my life. Now, sit back, read and judge for yourself if some of these situations were purely luck or perhaps, there really is a strong and sound basis to believe in miracles, performed by a much higher and more powerful force than we could ever imagine.

Before we get into the book, let me say, "Set your sights on the moon and even if you miss, you'll be among the stars." Set your goals to a certain height, and when you reach that, then set them higher. Set your goals to an attainable goal, and once reached, set them higher, and there is no way but up from that point forward.

If possible, let your occupation be something that you love, for then, it will not feel like working, and you will be happy.

I was sent to a mechanic and gunnery school, and after graduating as a BALL TURRET GUNNER, I was assigned to a bomber crew and ready to be sent to England to be part of the 8th Air Force. Our crew consisted of ten men: Pilot Elmer Gillespie, Co-Pilot Ted Chapman, Bombardier David Taylor, Navigator Hodge Mason, Top Turret (Engineer) Donald Zirbel, Radio Operator, Charlie McFall, Ball Turret Gunner, Elmer Eugene Browning, Waist Gunners, Tom Lambert and Robert Bush, and Tail Gunner Jeff Dickson.

We trained three months as a complete crew of ten in Dyersburg, Tennessee. Early April 1944, our crew was sent to Kearney, Nebraska to pick up a new B-17. We flew from there to Manchester, New Hampshire, then to Laborador and Iceland, across the North Atlantic Ocean to Belfast, Ireland. We left the plane there and went by ship across the Irish Sea to Scotland, then by train to a place called The Wash in England on the North Sea. From there, by train to Kettering, England, and by truck to Deenethorpe, 401st Bomb Group - 615th Squadron. Finally, we arrived at the 401st Bomb Group, Benefield, England. We became the newest crew in the 615th Squadron. After a short training period, we were put on flying status and ready for our first mission.

After a complete crew of ten, we flew thirty-five missions over Germany and enemy occupied France, Belgium and Holland. It took seven B-17's to complete our thirty-five missions. Our crew of ten had been assembled at Salt Lake Air Base in the outskirts of Salt Lake City, Utah.

We were sent to Dyersburg, Tennessee for final phase training as a full crew.

During this time, we would make flights, mostly at night with other B-17's to form a formation and pretend to be bombing the enemy. We ran these mock runs, and at one time, we

Dyersburg, Tennessee — just before going overseas to England

bombed Waco, Texas, as enemy territory (not really), but as a target test. That night, enroute back to Dyersburg, the fog socked in the base we were to return to, and some of our planes were lost. A couple even crashed, and our own B-17 had to land at a different Air Base. This was all practice in the United States before departing to our final destination.

Once we were in England, after every flight, we were met with paper cups and booze, once we were landed safely and the wounded or dead removed from the planes. The cups were large enough to hold a pint of whiskey, and we drank it straight.

When I talk about flak, it sounds like nothing, but flak was anti aircraft firing from the ground firing at us in the sky, and when we returned to our base without being shot down, we knew that God had once again smiled on us and brought us safely back to our base.

To say that we were not scared, would be leading you astray, for I am sure each man felt as I did, "Will this be my last mission, or will I be among the lucky ones to return to the base?"

It was scary for all of us, for most of us were nineteen, twenty, or so, very young men, just starting our future in life.

It was, however, a mission, each time that had to be done, and being true Americans, not wanting these attacks over American skies or the Germans to take over our country, we fought the best we could, and gave each mission everything that was inside us, drawing from inner strength that we were totally unaware that we possessed.

I can only say, those of us that survived, God had other plans for us.

I hope in someway that my trying to write about some of the events can help other young men and women to be brave and to fight for our country. If ever we needed young people to rally and take this country back from those who would destroy us, it is now.

For each of you, I pray God will give you the strength that HE gave to us to fight a war to keep our beautiful America safe, and our families.

MEET THE CREW

The crew consisted of Pilot Elmer Gillespie, Co-Pilot Theodore Chapman, up in the nose were Bombardier David Taylor and Navigator Hodge Mason. These four all were second Lieutenants. Engineer and Top Turret Gunner, Don Zirbel, Radio Operator Chuck McFall, Ball Turret Gunner Elmer (Gene) Browning, right waist Gunner Tom Lambert, left waist gunner Robert Bush, (no relation to George W. Bush) and last but not least, Tail Gunner Jeff Dickson. His full name was Jefferson Davis Dickson III; he was from Jackson, Mississippi, and a true rebel; he would take offense when an Englishman called him a Yankee, as they did all of us from the United States of America.

We were sent to Dyersburg, Tennessee for final phase training as a full crew. At the end of March, we went by train to Kearney, Nebraska where we were given a brand new B-17G for the beginning of our trip overseas. We flew to Manchester, New Hampshire and then up through Laborador and Iceland. After refueling our aircraft, we started our flight across the Atlantic Ocean. None of us had ever been that cold in our young lives. Finally, we landed in Ireland (about twelve miles from Belfast). We left our new plane there and went by ship across the Irish Sea to Glasgow, Scotland. From there, we went by train to a place called The Wash, on the east coast of England, right on the edge of the North Sea. We slept in tents while there and it was a far cry from the comfort of our barracks back in the states. After spending three days at The Wash, we finally got on a train and traveled to Kettering, England. At the train station, we were met by Army trucks; after climbing into the back of one truck, we were taken to Deenethorpe. This was the beginning of our months at the 401st Bomb Group - 615th Squadron. Before I start my list of missions, it would be better to relate a little about each member of our crew:

ELMER GILLESPIE - PILOT and main man: He was from Newton, Kansas, married. His wife's name was Margaret, and they had no children at that time. He had no trouble gaining the respect of 'HIS CREW'. After flying a few missions, we all agreed that he was the best pilot in the 401st Bomb Group.

THEODORE CHAPMAN - CO-PILOT, 2nd in command. He was from Rochester, New York. He was single and had

wanted to be a P-51 fighter pilot, but for some reason, he never passed the tests and so he ended up being a co-pilot on our crew. Although, he was real good at this job, he was not completely happy because of his failure at being a fighter pilot.

DAVID L. TAYLOR - BOMBARDIER.
From Amhurstdale, West Virginia. He
was married at the time, and his wife
was pregnant with their first child. He
was a compulsive poker player and always a big winner. On our sixth mission, he refused to fly again after returning to our base. More about the events
on this mission later in the book.

HODGE E. MASON - NAVIGATOR
(NICK NAME) "DEAD EYE". He
came from Monroe, Louisiana. After
getting better acquainted, we became
lifelong friends. He really became one
of the best navigators in our bomb
group. He often bragged about being a true REBEL, and if you got him
started, he talked about "Yankees versus Rebels," until he
finally ran out of material that he believed in.

T/SGT. DON D. ZIRBEL
ENGINEER AND TOP TURRET
GUNNER, directly behind the pilot and
co-pilot and in front of the Bomb-Bay.
He came from Newton, Iowa. He was
one shrewd operator and was real serious most of the time. We all knew that
we could depend on him when German

fighter planes attacked. He always seemed to be calm and
cool. I'm sure that the rest of our crew shared the same feelings that I felt, for he was one terrific individual.

21

T/SGT. CHARLIE A. MC FALL - RADIO OPERATOR. He came to us from Greenville, California. We all felt that he was as important as anyone could be. He did a great job sending and receiving messages that would be instrumental in our mission's safety completed and back to our 401st

bomb group. He and I became the best of friends. His primary object was to get all of our missions completed, so he could get back home and marry his sweetheart that he had met in Paducah, Kentucky at a U.S.O. dance. As I write this book today, in 2008, he and I are the only two living from our original ten man crew. Once, he and I went into town, and while walking down the street, we met two young ladies going in the opposite direction. I reached over in passing and pinched one on the buttocks. She immediately turned and told Chuck that she was not that kind of girl. Little did she know, we were not that kind of boys, MEN? Chuck

had no idea what she was talking about. I just shrugged my shoulders as if to say, "What did you do to them?"

S/SGT. ELMER E. BROWNING - BALL TURRET GUNNER.
I came to the crew from Danville, Illinois. My crew always called me Brownie. My crew and other people expressed their

feelings that this was the most hazardous position on the B-17. I guess because it hung outside the belly of our plane, and all the bombers B-17's and B-24's. It was the Loneliest spot that you could be in. Located directly behind the open bomb-bay doors when we were going toward our target. I always said that I had a bird's eye view of the ground and the bombs falling out of the shackles through the huge opening of the bomb-bay; as the bombardier would flip the toggle switch and say "Bombs Away". It was my job to protect the underside of our plane against enemy fighters that would attack from below. All of the crew wore electric heated suits over our flying coveralls to protect us from the unbearable cold. It would average minus 35 degrees at an altitude of 25,000 feet during the summer of 1944.

SGT. ROBERT BUSH - RIGHT WAIST GUNNER (No relationship to George W. Bush). He came to our crew from Apollo, Pennsylvania. He insisted on being called "Buck", and I have no idea why. He was the right waist gunner, and we all felt that his position was filled by an individual who could protect the plane from that side against German Fighter Planes. After our bombardier refused to fly anymore missions, Sgt. Bush took his place, and he was referred to as a toggeleer. His job was to push the toggle switch when he saw the other bombers drop their bombs without the use of a bomb site.

SGT. TOM LAMBERT - LEFT WAIST GUNNER. He came to the crew from McAllister, Oklahoma. His nick name was "Smokey Oakie". He never smoked anything but his crooked stem pipe. It was almost a permanent fixture. He would smoke it from the time we left the ground until we had to go on oxygen at 12,000 feet; then he would tap out the remaining ashes and refill with fresh tobacco and lay his pipe on the ledge beside his gun position, so it would be ready to light as soon as we would get down low enough to take off our oxygen masks. This showed he was an optimist. On one mission, a burst of flak knocked his pipe off the ledge and broke his pipe. He was  mad as hell. He had to tape it together when we got back to the base, as he could not find another pipe like that one. He was always calm even during heavy fighter attacks on the way to our target and back toward England.

SGT JEFF D. DICKSON -TAIL GUNNER. He came to the crew from Jackson, Mississippi. He was another Rebel and did not like to be called YANKEE by the English people. He was referred to as "The Kid". His full name was Jefferson Davis Dickson III and quite often, he told us that made him a true "dyed in the wool" Rebel. Jeff

was definitely an asset to our crew, and we all knew that the tail position would be completely covered during fighter attacks. He was a graduate from Armory School prior to joining the crew and was well versed in bombs and all kind of guns, explosives, and ammunition. The tail section was well covered by Jeff and his twin 50 caliber machine guns.

That covers the entire crew of "boys that became men" before our tour of duty ended on August 8, 1944.

Most of us became lifelong friends, for there was a brotherhood that held us together throughout our lifetimes. I am remembering that every young man on our crew did his job to keep us all safe.

When I arrived at our base, I noticed the hinge on the hanger door was manufactured in Danville, Illinois, at Allithprouty Corporation, where I had worked before joining the service. I also noticed Chuckles Candy was at the PX. This was also made in Danville, Illinois. Just goes to show you, how far our products from America traveled.

I will try to cover the high points of our missions over Germany and the enemy occupied countries in Europe. By being in aerial combat from April to August, we really learned to appreciate our beautiful UNITED STATES OF AMERICA. 1944 will always have a place in our hearts and minds, having flown all of our combat missions with the 401st bomb group - 615th squadron.

A messenger would come in the barracks and start calling out the pilot's names that were scheduled to fly that day. If our pilots name was called out, the entire crew would head for the mess hall. After eating breakfast, we went directly to briefing. The officers in charge would tell us what our mission would be, the bomb load, what the weather would be and what kind of defense guns we could expect. They would give us our time of take off and our ETA (estimated time of arrival) at the target. There would be a colored tape on the map showing the route to the target, and a different color tape showing the route back out. We went from briefing directly to the armorment building to get our gun barrels. We had to clean the excess oil from them and take them and install them in our gun position. After getting our guns ready, we would lay down on the ramp and relax until take off time.

In spite of what the movies show, we did not have a jeep to ride to the plane. We walked carrying our guns and equipment. We installed our guns in their positions and waited for the green flares to signal our take off. The green flares came from the control tower. We would immediately climb aboard the plane and wait in the radio room until we got off the ground. At that time, a bomber left the ground every thirty seconds. They would rendezvous in the air, each plane taking its place in the eighteen bomber formation to head for our target for the day.

The planes that completed the mission, after taxing into our parking area, we would then proceed to interrogation. Each crew would meet with an interrogator to tell him everything that happened during the mission. The interrogator would then make his report to our group commander. Each gunner would take his guns back to the armorment shack and oil and clean them and put them in a gun barrel sock. We would put our gun barrel sock always in the same place. They belonged to us and were never to be used by another crew member. Every gunner was responsible for his own gun barrel. We took care of them because they meant life or death to us.

We were then free to return to our barracks to do what we wanted to do until chow time. To me, personally, a good HOT shower always felt wonderful at that time. Also, a visit to the latrine was also welcome after being in the air six to eight hours or sometimes more. We always welcomed care packages from home and would share with other members of the crew.

Gulfport, Mississippi — Aircraft Mechanic School, 1943

MISSIONS OVER GERMANY AND ENEMY OCCUPIED COUNTRIES AND TERRITORIES 1944

German railroad destroyed 1944

#1 Lyons, April 30, 1944

Our first mission was later referred to as a "milk run" because we never met any enemy fighters and the flak did very little damage. We had a great escort of P-51's and P-47's. We were really happy to report that our target was knocked out completely and also glad that we had drawn an easy mission to start our tour of duty in the ETO. (European Theatre of Operation)

#2 Berlin, May 4, 1944

We crossed the North Sea and the coast of Germany. Before we were very deep into Germany, the strangest thing happened; the ball turret is probably the loneliest place to be in the plane. Above the roar of the four huge engines, I began hearing the most beautiful harp music. I don't know how long it lasted or if it was a figment of my imagination, but at the time, it was as plain as anything I have ever heard. The radio operator received a message from 8th Air Force Headquarters to cancel that mission and bomb the secondary target in Holland, due to weather conditions over Berlin. At that very instant, the music stopped, and I never heard it again. We went on to bomb a German Airdrome with very good results. We destroyed a lot of German fighter planes on the ground in Amsterdam. We were hit by flak as we passed over the target, but very little damage to our squadron. We returned to our base where our ground crew patched several small holes. Three days of rest, then Berlin was scheduled again.

#3 Berlin, May 7, 1944

We started back across the southern part of the North Sea with real good weather. As we crossed the coast, the ceiling closed in. We had a lot of flak all the way to Berlin. At one time, it looked thick enough to let our wheels down and roll on it. We dropped our bombs through a heavy overcast and so there was no way to see the results. The right waist gunner had a small burn on one foot due to a faulty heated shoe. This time, our ground crew had a lot of holes to patch.

#4 Berlin, May 8, 1944

We were briefed for Trier, but the plans changed after take off. Once again, we hit Berlin, and from the coast to the target, we were hit by heavy flak. When we returned to our base, we found several holes in the fuselage that showed the ground crew the kind of mission we had flown. One of them good-naturedly started giving me hell for getting their plane shot up. Then when I told him that he could take my place the next time, he immediately changed his tune and in no uncertain terms, said, "NO WAY!" He would rather stay in England where it was safe.

#5 Luxenburg, May 9, 1944

I was called out to fly with another crew and found that our radio operator would be flying with the same crew. We had very little opposition. For this, we were really thankful. I'm sure that Chuck was as nervous as I was, flying with a crew that we knew nothing about. Flak hit the low element, but we had very little damage to the plane that we were in. The worst part for me was the fact that their ground crew had not checked the turret prior to take-off, and it would start turning as soon as I turned on the power. I was upset by this, and I had to continually keep moving the control handles to off-set creeping, as we called it. You can bet that I told their ground crew of the slip shod way they serviced this aircraft. Chuck and I were both happy to be back with our crew which we had complete confidence in their ability to perform and work as an expert crew.

#6 Merseburg, May 12, 1944

We were late taking off, but this proved to be our WORST mission to date. We ran into intense and accurate flak as soon as we got over enemy territory. Before we got to the target, we received a direct hit in the nose section of our plane. A piece of flak fragment hit a portable oxygen bottle causing it to become a missile, and the bombardier and navigator were busy trying to dodge the bottle as it flew around the nose like a balloon released filled with air. This filled the compartment with black smoke that was blown all through the plane. From all of the commotion, we just knew that our two men in that area were hurt badly. When things settled down, we found that they were both alright but shaken from their ordeal. We were over the target a short time later, and when the bombardier pushed the toggle switch to drop our load with his familiar voice, "Bombs Away", nothing happened and we realized our bomb release cables had been cut by the flak burst. We had to take screw drivers to release the locking device that held each bomb securely to the shackles. The top turret gunner was hold-ing the parachute harness tightly to keep the bombardier from falling out of the bomb-bay. We lost our bombardier after this mission. His nerves were shattered from this ordeal, and he refused to fly anymore. Later, during the way, he was given a somewhat less than an honorable discharge. Some of the crew made remarks that they thought he was "yellow", but I always maintained that it could have happened to any of us. Anyway, we returned to our base with a plane shot full of holes. No other injuries. I received my FIRST AIR MEDAL.

#7 Kiel, May 19, 1944

We were briefed for another mission to Berlin. Due to bad weather, we were told to hit our secondary target. We ran into intense and accurate flak, but we returned to our base with just a few holes in our plane. Some of the other planes were shot-up pretty bad. They had not faired as well as us, although there was considerable damage to some of our eighteen planes, we all came back with no casualties. Up to this point, we had not had any contact with enemy fighters, but we knew that it would just be a matter of time until all hell would break loose.

#8 Bayon - Blainvillie, May 23, 1944

Once again, we had been a part of an early morning take-off to bomb strategic railroad marshalling yards. As we flew over the enemy coast, we encountered light to heavy flak. It was fairly sporadic and a lot of it was falling way short of our bomb group formation. We did get a few pieces coming through our fuselage, but the only one that even came close to any of our crew, was a pretty good chunk that lodged right beneath the co-pilot. He said that it came close enough that he felt the impact of it when it came through the thin aluminum and bounced off the bottom of his seat.

#9 Metz-Fecamp, May 25, 1944

We took off to bomb another important railroad marshalling yard. This was where the German Personnel would assemble their trains to carry ammunition and other supplies to the troops that were stationed at various locations in Germany and enemy occupied countries. This was another "milk run" for our group, but flak was heavy directly behind us where another group of B-17's was following us. That group was hit hard, and we saw one plane go down out of formation. We counted seven parachutes come out of that plane. We never found out what happened to the other three that did not bail out. Our tail gunner was the only one in our crew that had a problem. He got frost bite on the right cheek from having his oxygen mask too tight. He spent a few days in the base hospital but rejoined the crew on June 2nd. We all had one day off to rest. It was most welcome.

#10 Ludwig shaven - May 27, 1944

This was a mission to REMEMBER. Extremely heavy flak that seemed to blot out the sun. One thing that was in our favor, we had a beautiful escort of P-51's and P-47's. We could see them engaged in battle with German fighter planes. There were several enemy planes shot down but none of ours were lost. Of course, we were thankful that our "Little Brothers" were there to keep them away from us. Our group returned to our base without firing a shot. We had saved our ammunition to use at a later day, not knowing that it would be tomorrow and our biggest battle up to this time of our flying career.

#11 Desseau - May 29, 1944

This day started with a later than usual take off. We fully expected another easy mission by it being so late getting off the ground. When we went to briefing, we were told that our target for today would be a JU88 fighter factory. For the mission, we had a replacement tail gunner, and I never even got to hear his name. He told me that he didn't have a flak helmet, so I gave him mine because I didn't have room for it down in the ball turret anyway. He was sent to us to take the place of Jeff Dickson who was still in the hospital recovering from facial frost bite.

Once we arrived over the coast of Germany, we were hit by extremely heavy flak all the way to our target and for quite a long way back to the enemy coast. German fighters came at our group before we got to the target and even as our bombs fell toward the ground. Our air battle lasted for an hour and a half. We came close to running out of ammunition. It was estimated that we were hit by three hundred German fighter planes that came at our formation from eleven, twelve, and one o'clock high low and level. Our replacement tail gunner was hit by an exploding twenty mil shot by an ME109 that came right through our formation. The fragments hit him in the back of the head. It knocked him out, and when he revived, he stayed back in the tail firing his twin fifty caliber machine guns until the battle was over. Had it not been for the flak helmet, he would have been killed for sure. The helmet was completely blown off his head and ruined.

There were eighteen bombers left our base that morning, and only eight made it back to England. We were hit from all directions by JU88's, ME109's, ME210's, and FW190's. Some crews managed to bail out and others were killed when their planes exploded from direct hits of flak and/or German fighter planes. When we were back over the English Channel, the tail gunner crawled back up to the radio room bleeding profusely from his head wounds. I came up out of the Ball Turret and gave him a shot of morphine and sprinkled sulfa powder to stop the bleeding. He had lost a lot of blood from the back of his head. When calmed down from the shot, I wrapped him in a blanket, and he lay in the radio room until we landed at our base.

As we approached our base, the co-pilot fired a red flare to show that we had a wounded aboard. We were not the only ones that fired flares, so there were several ambulances that came out to meet each plane. The other seven B-17's that made it back, had wounded or dead crew members aboard. The tail gunner had five fragments removed from his head and by the Grace of God, he survived. I went to visit him in the base hospital and jokingly said, "When you get out of here, you owe me a new flak helmet."

I always carried my flak helmet with me to the plane for a mission, but I never wore it, as there just was not enough space for me to put it on my head while in the ball turret.

Our Bomb Group was credited with one hundred and fifty German fighter planes shot down, but we paid a very high price in having lost ten of our B-17's and complete crews. Besides, the "killed in action" crew members that were brought back to our base in the eight heavily damaged planes that made it back. We were a sad bunch of men that evening. We didn't do any celebrating over the destruction of the target that we had been sent to hit.

#12 Alprech - Equiben - June 1, 1944

After a nice three day rest, once again, we were called to fly. This was another "milk run", for this, we were all extremely grateful. The target was on the coast of France. We bombed through a heavy overcast, so we could not see the results. After landing at our base, I was awarded my very first OAK LEAF CLUSTER to go on my AIR MEDAL.

#13 Neufchatel - June 3, 1944

How could we be so lucky to have two "milk runs" back to back? Once again, we dropped our bombs through a heavy overcast, so the results could not be seen. We did see a little flak off in the distance, but none even close to our group. When we returned to our base, we all agreed that #13 was not unlucky!

#14 Paris - Massey/Palaiseau - June 4, 1944

We were hit by a lot of flak all the way to the target and back to the coast of France and the English Channel. We had received a lot of damage from the flak bursts that caused us to make a forced landing at a fighter base in England. The damage was repaired over night, and we were able to return to our base the next morning. The night of June 5th, the tail gunner, Jeff Dickson, and I went into Kettering, and I guess that we tried to drink all of the Pubs dry. We caught the last bus, 11:00 PM, back to our base. The First Sergeant from our base operations happened to be sitting across the aisle in the bus. He asked me if our crew was scheduled to fly the next day, because there was a lot of activity at the mess hall. I said, "I didn't know", but Jeff and I got off the bus and went inside. Sure enough, the rest of our crew was there eating breakfast, and wondered where we were. We just had time for coffee and head for the briefing room.

D - DAY

#15 Caen - June 6, 1944

Needless to say, Jeff and I both sobered up real quick when we saw that the target was to bomb ahead of our troops that would be embarking from landing crafts for the first wave to hit the beach for the big push of the INVASION OF EUROPE. We lost one B-17 from our group as we flew through heavy flak from the German defenders against the invasion. There was a tremendous amount of blood shed as our troops stormed the beach on this fateful day that will go down in HISTORY. All ten crew members of the stricken bomber were picked up out of the English Channel and returned to our base. Their spirits were dampened from landing in the water, but they were very happy to be picked up by a ship that was carrying part of the invasion force to the French Coast. That was one day that I was happy to be in one of the B-17's instead of one of our men that were rushing the beach that day. So many lost their lives.

#16 Bernay St. Martin (Rene') - June 11, 1944

We were called out at midnight for an early mission. It is what we referred to as another "milk run". There was very little flak which was low and "almost" harmless. We did return to our base with a couple of holes in our plane. We were happy to have destroyed a pretty good number of German Aircraft at this Airdrome in Northern France. This was an important place for the German planes to take off from to bomb and strike our troops. We caught them by surprise because there was not a single plane able to get off the ground when we made our bomb run.

#17 Vitry - En - Artuis - June 12, 1944

This was another early take off to hit a vital German airdrome. It was a beautiful day with clear weather, so we were hit by heavy flak before, during and after our bomb run. The ground crew had very little repair work to get the plane ready for the next mission. When we landed back to our bomb group, the results of our mission showed that we had completely destroyed this airfield and most of the German fighter planes on the ground. Needless to say, our interrogation officer was very happy and went on to report it to our group commander, Col. Bowman, and in turn to our squadron C.O.

I know that in 1984 and 1985 Col. Bowman was the President of the 401st Bombardment Group (H) Association, Inc. "Best Damned Outfit in the USAAF". He was a retired Brig. Gen. H. W. Bowman. Believe it or not, I lived on Bowman Avenue in Danville, Illinois. I sent in a photo of our crew, and it was put on their mailer December 12, 1985: CREW OF "Elmer's Tune", kneeling (L to R): Jeff Dickson, Elmer Browning, Elmer Gillespie, David Taylor, and Ted Chapman. Standing (L to R): Bob Bush, Tom Lambert, Chas. McFall, Don Zirbel, and Hodge Mason. It was the Christmas Issue, and just the photo and the name of our crew appeared in this mail out.

#18 Le Bourget - June 14, 1944

At this time, this was the largest force of heavy bombers in the History of the 8th Air Force to take off on a single mission. We hit a very heavy amount of flak at the target area and all the way back to the coast. We lost two B-17's from our squadron. Several parachutes were seen coming from these planes, and we can only assume that they were captured when they hit the ground. Our plane returned to our base with several flak holes, but we felt fortunate that we had not met any German fighters. When we landed at our base and went through interrogation, cleared and stored our gun barrels, then I went to our great barracks, to find that I had received my second OAK LEAF CLUSTER to be added to my AIR MEDAL.

#19 Hamburg - June 18, 1944

Our crew was called out at midnight for an early take off. At briefing, when showed what our target would be, you could hear everyone groan. We were told to knock out the German oil refinery just south of the Kiel Canal.

We crossed the North Sea, never quite knowing when German fighters would venture out over the water. Their coast was thick with radar installations, so they always seemed to know where we were headed.

We ran into heavy intense flak as soon as we flew across the German coast. At this kind of target, we were loaded with incendiary bombs. They would create heavy damage by all of the fires that would be started when the bombs hit oil or fuel storage tanks. As we flew over the Kiel Canal, I saw flashes of guns firing from a battle ship anchored there. I called the pilot and told him that I was going to fire a few rounds back at them. When he gave me the OK, I aimed my twin 50's and raked the length of that ship. I really don't know whether I hit anyone or not, but their guns quit shooting at us. We still had heavy flak all the way to our target. Being down in the ball turret, I had a good view of the bombs hitting the ground. As we turned back over the North Sea, I could see a lot of fire and black smoke created by direct hits. We reported our success to the interrogating officer, and I went back to our barracks and went to bed. It had been a very long day, and I was very tired, not only in body, but in spirit. It was times like this that I would think of Helen and wish that I could hold her close to me and tell her just how much I loved her and how very proud I was of her. When my mind and body was tired from the stress of being in the ball turret watching and waiting to be attacked, it was the image of her and our sweet love that helped me to go to sleep at night and relax. I suppose we all had that "special" someone back home that made the fighting worth while. I know that I had several "special" some ones, Helen, my father, Florence, my two sisters and friends. I felt that what I was doing was somehow protecting them, and I know it was, for WE DID WIN THE WAR.

Most of us did not worry so much about ourselves. We worried about our loved ones back home and what their reaction would be if they received a telegram. All of us had a lot of concern for the people we loved so very much back in America.

#20 Bordeaux/Merignac - June 19, 1944

This was another early call out. We were again greeted with heavy flak all the way from the French coast to our target; which happened to be another German occupied airfield. We fully expected to encounter a lot of enemy fighter planes, but we were lucky, the target was clear of any clouds, so we could see that our bombs completely destroyed the planes on the ground as well as all of the buildings in the area. Our formation flew West out over the Atlantic Ocean to get out of range of the big guns on the ground. We ran into extremely bad weather out over the ocean, and we came close to several mid air collisions in breaking up the formation. Our pilot flew down so low that I was getting spray from the ocean all over my ball turret. We were down almost under water. I remember telling the pilot to raise it up a little bit that I did not want to be in a submarine. We arrived back at our base with a lot of damage by flak and once again the ground crew had a few choice words about not taking better care of their plane. We were thankful

That there were no casualties.

#21 Fienvillers - June 23, 1944

This was another fairly easy trip. Of course, we were hit by the usual flak over the target area, but there were no fighter plane attacks. We decided that this was another "milk run", although we did have a few holes in our plane, for our ground crew to repair before the next mission. By this time, they were getting to the point of expecting the damage so they did not complain. They just thanked us for bringing their plane back home. We were too late for dinner and too early for supper, and we just had to wait for our evening chow. You can bet we were all ready to eat when we got to the mess hall.

#22 Belloy Sur-Somine-Bachimon-June 24, 1944

We were called later than any other time, so we were expecting an easy mission. There was heavy and accurate flak from the time we flew over the coast all the way to our target. Sometime, before we got to the target, our left waist gunner had the urge for a bowel movement, so he used a cardboard box and placed it down in the camera well just below the radio operator. Wouldn't you know that shortly after placing the box there, we received a burst of flak directly in that area? The main force of shrapnel went out of the right side of the radio room, missing our radio operator, but it knocked out my fourteen inch sight window, and I caught the contents of that box all over me. Later on, I would say that I was the only guy in the 8th Air Force that was shot at and crapped on at the same time. This blast also knocked out our intercom system, so I had to wait until we got back to our base to give Bush a few choice words. Our ground crew had a lot of repair work to do including the installing of a new sight window as well as the mess in my turret to be cleaned.

The B-17's did not have bathrooms, and we had a relief tube that had a little funnel inside for urine, but to my knowledge, that was the only time any crew member had to do the other job.

#23 Mont artier - June 24, 1944

We were called out to fly again before we got to sleep, so we were pretty tired. It was a long flight, mostly over water, but we were hit by heavy flak on the coast of France, but even as much flak that was shot at us, we had very little damage to our plane. Just a few patches to cover the holes. Other planes in our group did not come back as lucky as we.

#24 Laon - Couvpon - June 28, 1944

Again, we left our base early to bomb a German airdrome. We had an awful lot of flak all the way to the target area. Our plane sustained a lot of damage but no casualties. We landed at a B-24 base to have minor repairs. That day, the base where we landed had just lost one complete squadron consisting of six B-24's. There were more B-17's landed there than their own planes. They were pretty devastated over their lost planes as well as the complete crews.

The repair work was completed by morning, so we left there and landed back at our base about noon. Our friends were glad to see us. I received another **OAK LEAF CLUSTER.**

#25 Leipzig - July 7, 1944

We were called out early again after having a nice long rest period. This highly appreciated rest was just what our crew needed, for this was one of our roughest missions along with Hamburg and Desseau. Again, my ball turret took a beating from the German anti-aircraft gunners. It seemed as though they knew exactly what altitude we would be flying. The flak was thick and heavy as well as being highly accurate. Several of the small side windows were shot out besides the large piece of flak that came through the metal part and lodged close to my head. Whether it was one bad shot or maybe, they didn't know how to spell my name, anyway, I was thankful for whatever reason they missed me. I was in no mood to receive the **FAMOUS PURPLE HEART** medal. When we got back to our barracks, a corporal came in calling my name and said that I was wanted at Group headquarters and to be there in ten minutes. I wondered what I had done to be called in on the carpet. When I arrived in the office, I found five others there in class "A" uniforms. We only had to wait about five minutes to find out why we were called to headquarters. Three of them received a **PURPLE HEART** medal. One was presented with the **BRONZE STAR,** and two of us had a beautiful **DISTIN-GUISHED FLYING CROSS** pinned to our uniforms by our

401st Bomb Group Commander Col. Bowman. **This was truly ONE of the PROUDEST DAYS OF MY LIFE.** A few days before that, we had been told that our tour of duty had been increased to thirty missions instead of twenty-five. After a few days, we were put back on flying status.

#26 Munich - July 13, 1944

While our crew was not flying, the 401st group made two trips to Munich but today, we were included in the eighteen bombers to go back. We were hit by heavy flak and also some rockets as we got close to the target. After dropping our bombs and starting back toward England, we were attacked by German fighter planes. "They came at us about twelve in each group right out of the sun, so we did not see them until they made the first pass." This quoted by me to the associated press when we made it back to our base. "It was quite an air battle, but fortunately, we only lost one bomber, but we did shoot down four of their ME109's. The damage to our plane was from the flak that we had run into at the target. We did not get a count on the parachutes that came out of the stricken planes that we lost, but thought, maybe, all nine men got out. Just to be captured by the German soldiers when they hit the ground."

#27 Schweinfurt - July 21, 1944

Once again, we were faced with heavy flak over the target area and all the way back to the coast. Every bomber in our group arrived back to our base with flak damage. Some had more damage than others. We did not meet any German fighters because we had met a group of P-51's and P-47's to escort us back to the English side of the channel.

As we crossed the English Coast, I pushed my control handles forward which moved by twin 50 caliber machine guns straight down, and the hatch of my turret was in position, so that I could climb up inside the plane into the waist gunner's area. I had been down in that cramped up position for so long that day, and I needed to get out of it to stretch.

Along with the cramped position, I felt pretty stressed out from all of the flak that we had been hit with and after stretching, I crawled back down into the turret to clear my guns to prepare for landing. Without thinking, I did not hook my safety belt. There wasn't enough room in the ball turret to wear a parachute, so I wore a safety belt in case I had to bail out, I could climb back into the plane, and grab my parachute and hook it to my safety belt. This time, I closed the hatch, turned on the power and rolled the turret down in flying position. I pulled the charging handles, raised the cover to clear the ammunition from the guns. I was getting short of breath, so I leaned back to rest. Without any warning, the hatch snapped open, and it took every bit of strength to hold on. After what seemed like an eternity, I had a strange sensation as if a huge hand had pushed against my back and into the safety of my turret. At that time, I quickly rolled the turret back into position, so that I could get back into the plane.

The hatch was so badly twisted and bent that the ground crew had to replace it as well as several places to patch created by flak damage.

#28 St. Lo - July 24, 1944

We took off with a load of anti personal fragmentation bombs to bomb ahead of our advancing infantry to clear out the German defenders, or at least to make it a little easier for them to move up and take prisoners. It didn't help matters though, because the clouds gathered over the target area, and we could not drop our bombs for **FEAR** of hitting our own troops. We also ran into heavy flak in this area, so we carried our bomb load back to our base. We did not like to do this because we felt that we had let our troops down completely.

#29 St. Lo - July 25, 1944

We had orders to go back today and do our job right. This time, the weather was clear and a line of smoke showed us where our troops were located. We carried the same bomb load that we had the day before and we did drop them where they did the most good for our troops. Not the first flak burst today, so our bombing results were almost perfect.

#30 Munich - July 31, 1944

Once again, we took off to bomb one of our most dreaded targets. We reached our IP (initial point), and our right inboard engine was hit by flak causing oil to be spilled all over the right wing. Our pilot, Elmer Gillespie, quickly feathered the prop to keep it from flying apart as it had started into a windmill action. We were falling behind our formation, so our pilot decided that we should open the bomb-bay doors and salvo our bomb load. The bomb-bay doors closed, and we felt a little better getting rid of the load that could blow us out of the sky with a direct flak hit in that section. We made a big turn and started back toward England alone. We had barely leveled off to start back when flak hit our left outboard engine. This explosion almost tore that engine apart.

About ten minutes later, our right outboard engine began to vibrate badly due to the super charger being hit. By this time, we were about half way between Brussels and the coast. The pilot called me out of my gun position and told me to make preparations to break the ball turret loose to get as much weight out of our plane, so we would stand a better chance of making it back across the Channel. By using one of the gun barrels from the waist gun, the turret finally broke loose and fell into the English Channel. The radio operator knowing what could happen, had positioned himself behind me and held onto my parachute harness to keep me from being sucked out of the huge opening where the turret had been. The rest of our crew had been busy throwing everything out that could be torn loose. Halfway across the Channel, the right out board engine quit. That just left us with one good engine running. We positioned ourselves in the radio room in case our pilot would have to ditch the plane in the Channel. We were flying real close to the water when Chuck, the radio operator, yelled at us and said, "We are about to fly over the White Cliffs of Dover." Our luck had not run out because there was an expanded metal runway just ahead. With wheels down, our pilot brought our crippled **FORTRESS** in and landed as if it had four engines running. As our plane rolled to a stop, our last engine quit running because it had been over worked to get us back. About that time, the C.O. of the fighter base pulled up in a jeep and yelled at our pilot to get that "damn" thing off my runway; so his fighter planes could land. After our pilot told him that it had gone as far as it could and after the C.O. saw how badly damaged our plane was, he said, "My God man, how did you ever bring it back?" Our pilot calmly replied, "The Good Lord extended His hand to help." After making a few phone calls to the

401st Bomb Group, they sent a heavily patched B-17 down to get us. It was named "The Bad Penny." It had lived up to its name by always returning.

We arrived back at our base late that evening. When I walked into our barracks, I yelled, "Alright, put all my things back - I'm home!" Everyone was happy to see that we had all made it back alive because at interrogation, we had been reported as missing in action. Our crew all had thought that our pilot should have been awarded a higher medal than the Distinguished Flying Cross.

#31 Nienburg - August 5, 1944

One more mission classed as a "milk run" with very little flak and no German fighter attacks. We did see a few rockets fired at us, but they were not accurate, so we returned to our base without the usual damage. Needless to say, we were extremely happy after surviving our previous mission on July 31, 1944.

#32 Caen - Hautmensnil - August 8, 1944

We took off this morning with a full load of anti-personnel bomb clusters to hit the enemy lines that had the British infantry pinned down. Hopefully, this would allow them to push farther toward Germany. We hit heavy flak over our target area and our future didn't look too bright for awhile. This mission completed our tour of duty in the E.T.O. (European Theatre of Operation)

Turret Gunner Presented DFC

Staff Sgt. Elmer E. Browning, husband of Mrs. Helen Browning, 802 Martin St., and son of Mr. and Mrs. Ralph Browning of Westville, has been awarded the Distinguished Flying Cross in England.

The citation accompanying the award reads: "For extraordinary achievement while serving as ball turret gunner of a Flying Fortress on a number of combat bombardment missions over Germany and enemy occupied Europe. Displaying great courage and skill, Sergeant Browning, fighting from his gun position has warded off many enemy attacks and has materially aided in each of these missions. The courage, coolness and skill displayed by the sergeant on all these occasions reflect the highest credit upon himself and the armed forces of the U. S."

He also holds the Air Medal with three Oak Leaf Clusters.

Local Flier In Reich Raid

Sgt. Elmer Browning of Danville, a ball turret gunner, was in the crew of one of the thousand American bombers which pounded Munich and Saarbrucken, a major steel and coal center on the western German border.

Commenting on the German air force opposition in the Saarbrucken attack, Browning is quoted as follows by the Associated Press:

"We received four direct hits from Messerschmitt — 109s and Focke-Wulf 190s which came in waves of 10 to 12. They came out of the sun and hit us almost before we had a chance to see them."

GENERAL ORDERS)
NUMBER   215)

Hq 1st Bombardment Division,
E X T R A C T   APO 557. 3 August 1944.

I. Under the provisions of Army Regulations 600-45, 22 September 1943, as amended, and pursuant to authority contained in letter, Hq Eighth Air Force, File 200.6, 1 June 1944, subject, "Awards and Decorations", the DISTINGUISHED FLYING CROSS is awarded to the following-named Officers and Enlisted Men, for extraordinary achievement, as set forth in citation.

*   *   *   *   *   *

ELMER E. BROWNING, 36448151, Staff Sergeant, 615th Bombardment Squadron, 401st Bombardment Group (H), Army Air Forces, United States Army. For extraordinary achievement while serving as Ball Turret Gunner of a B-17 airplane on a number of combat bombardment missions over Germany and German occupied countries. Home address: 802 Martin Street, Danville, Illinois.

*   *   *   *

By Command of Major General WILLIAMS:

BARTLETT BEAMAN,
Brigadier General, U. S. Army,
Chief of Staff.

OFFICIAL:
ROBERTS P. JOHNSON, JR.,
Lt. Colonel, A.G.D.,
Adjutant General.

51

The Elmer Eugene Browning Family
Helen (my wife of over 50 years) — Elmer Eugene
Sheila (our only child)

HOME AGAIN

We were given credit of three non combat missions for some of the flights that we made over the English Channel looking for survivors of aircraft that had been damaged and reported to have been forced to ditch unable to make it back to England. These three credits allowed us thirty-five missions as listed on the back of our Honorable Discharge.

It may seem as if I have played down these missions that we called, "Milk Runs". There were crew members in our formation that were getting hit. Later on, I found out the 8th Air Force lost more men than the Marine's lost in World War II.

Flak was something in which there was no defense against, and there were times, we would have welcomed German fighters to have something to shoot to defend ourselves.

By 1944, the German anti aircraft gunners on the ground had a lot of practice at shooting at Air Force formations. That was why we dreaded the flak more than German fighter planes. We never knew when one of their shells would find our plane with a direct hit.

August 8, 1944 - My wife, Helen's 18th birthday. Our last mission.

This was the end of the old crew #10 that had flown all of their missions with the 401sat Bomb Group - 615th Squadron, part of the MIGHTY EIGHTH AIR FORCE. After we were all through flying, we finally realized that it took seven B-17's for us to complete our tour of duty out of Deenethoppe Air Base in England. The German airmen and the anti-aircraft gunners were responsible for shooting a lot of holes in our planes before we were through. They did not hit any of our original crew members and did not knock any of our seven planes out of the sky. We feel that our crew did our part to winning the war in Europe.

I left the Bomb Group September 8th and arrived back in THE GOOD OLD U.S.A. and on October 8th, after spending a month at a replacement depot awaiting orders to go home, we came back across the Atlantic Ocean in style; aboard The Queen Mary. After checking in at Camp Shanks, we were given an all night pass to New York City. There were three of us together from Illinois that went into the City to celebrate, Don Martin, Fred Cope and myself. As you can imagine, we really hung one on that night.

Late the following day, we were issued traveling orders and went by train to Chicago, checked in at the Ft. Sheridan, where we were given a fifteen day delay-in-route. I arrived in Danville, Illinois on the C&E.I railroad at 12:35 AM on Friday, October 13, 1944.

I had sent Helen a wire from Chicago stating that I had arrived back in the United States. To my surprise, she was waiting at the train station. I asked how she knew to meet me, and she laughingly said, "I read where the wire came from, and it said, Chicago, so I knew that you would be here on the next train." She was big as a barrel, as our little girl was born the next month on Thanksgiving Day. This did not keep us from doing what all young lovers do when they have been apart. We were both so happy to see each other, and even with the large stomach, Sheila, my Helen still fit in my arms very nicely.

I don't know what I would have done with out a woman like Helen who helped me so much when I came back from the war to adapt to civilian life after seeing thousands killed. Knowing every time our crew got in that B-17 that we might never return. Worrying about my young wife, pregnant, in America. Loving my country, and our crew, and knowing that we all depended on each of us doing our jobs in order to remain alive, as well as knowing that a power much higher than us stood guard over us to bring us back safely home to America.

My greatest concern of being killed in action was the thought of Helen being left a widow with a baby to raise. I know that she went through so very much while I was trying to do my part to keep America free. She went through her only pregnancy without me, and the delivery of our only child, Sheila.

Helen lived with her mother and father most of the time that I was gone, but her father and her did not get along very well, because of her father being an alcoholic. Helen became very serious about life. Her home life contributed to a negative attitude, so to keep things in check, I played games and laughed a lot with our little daughter, and it became a way of escape for us and helped us to both love life and lots of laughter.

Helen had low self esteem, and we all have that to a certain degree when young. When she was pregnant with Sheila and not knowing if her husband would return from the war created some unhappy moments for her. I know she was lonely, and wanting her husband and her own place.

When I returned from the service after not passing the physical, it was hard to find a decent job. My sister, Lorene, had an apartment, and she moved to Florida, so Helen rented the apartment for twenty-five dollars a month, and her allotment check was only fifty dollars a month. This did include all bills paid and was furnished. We lived there when I came home, an upstairs apartment. It was an old house with three apartments upstairs. All three apartments used the same bathroom down the hall, and each apartment had a small bedroom, living room and tiny kitchen. We were only able to live there about three or four months after I returned from the war, as I was without a job. We lived with her mother and dad a little while, and then we got a government apartment on the East end of town. Later, we bought a 14 x 20 garage from Sears and moved it to Helen's father's property. We lived in it for about two years. We had run one electrical line over to the building and it had one single light in the ceiling. We used her parent's bathroom. When I got out of service, I did have 40% disability from my loss of hearing and received finally about $120 a month, and then I went to work for the Chevrolet Dealer making $1.16 an hour.

Later, we bought a prefab house for $6,000.00, and we had to pay $600.00 down and $42.00 per month. I bought a space heater that used oil and installed it myself in the front room. Later, we bought a furnace, and I installed it, as I could not afford to have it installed. Then I got another job cleaning out coal cars for the New York Central, and it was a dirty, filthy job, and I only worked there a few months, then I got a job driving a Pepsi Cola truck. Then with the help of a friend, I was hired as a welder at Hyster, and I got my GED and went to night school, then promotions came faster, and I was made a supervisor. I was making $3500.00 a month when I retired at age sixty-two. After scraping and scratching all those years, I took the early retirement and had done pretty well and had made a decent living for my wife and daughter. I was never sorry that I retired, as it gave me a few years with my wife before she died, and we had some good times together. When I made foreman, I was making $625.00 per month, and my boss gave me a fifty dollar a month raise in just a few weeks and a few months later, he gave me a hundred dollar a month raise. I had been through some hard times and worked long hours, but we managed to get by and in spite of the long hard hours, I was HAPPY, and I believe my wife and daughter were happy

I am grateful that God gave me the courage to finish all thirty-five missions with the wonderful crew. None of us knew if we would make it home again or not. We all were so very young. We needed to be young in order to hold up physically to the cold, the task of defending our country and the world. It took a lot of stamina.

I watched the movie, the Memphis Belle, and I know that it was a movie based on fact, however it was a movie. I do have the government release of this movie. I also know that the ten man crew did NOT fuss and fight, for each depended on the other to do their job, and we were all too close to fuss and fight. I also know that no one removed their oxygen mask to talk, for the lack of oxygen would have killed us, for there was no oxygen at that altitude, but then how could they have talked without removing their oxygen mask? We were able to communicate via throat mikes.

A B-17 was not pressurized like the modern day aircraft. Without oxygen mask, death would come in just a few seconds, because our brain would have been deprived of oxygen which was necessary to sustain our life. It would have been a painless death, as we were taught in our training program. It is an absolute necessity for oxygen to get to the brain, because it is necessary to sustain life at that altitude.

Also, the last mission made by the Memphis Belle, the government release, showed the Queen of England came out and personally shook the hand of each member of the crew.

When we went to England, we were to do twenty-five missions also, but after we flew our twenty-five missions, the government extended us for five more missions, and after thirty missions, they extended us for five more.

I did not know then that 8th Air Force had lost more men than the Marines. That was a surprise when I read that, for the marines were usually the first to storm the beaches.

All of these men had a very special place in my heart, and I shall never forget any of them. I am thankful that Chuck is still alive, and I can stay in contact with him. I love him like a brother. He married his Martha, and she too is still living. They have been married over sixty years.

When Melba and I went to Texas last summer to meet her brothers and family, we went by and had lunch with Chuck. He looked good, and told me to marry Melba, so I followed his advise, as he always gave good advise.

After about my third mission, I found that one of my teachers from high school, Frank Rodgers, was at the same base in England that I was, and the way I found him, Jeff and I had gone to the post theater, and I saw this guy climb onto the stage. I said, "Boy, I know that walk." When he climbed off stage, it was Frank Rodgers and after the show was over, Jeff and I started around to the stage door to catch him. He came out with a group and got on his bicycle and started to ride away, but he turned and looked at me and recognized me and came over to where I was to find out if I was with the Engineers. I told him I was a gunner on a bomber crew. From that day forward, he was at the flight line when we took off and when we came back. It was a wonderful feeling to see someone from home, and to know that they cared enough about me to see us leave and return from our missions.

After my furlough was over in Danville, Illinois, I was to report for 'R AND R", rest and recuperation, down at Miami Beach, Florida. Don Martin and Fred Cope were also to report there, so we met in Jacksonville, Illinois and drove down in Don's car. We were booked in at the Hotel Traymore right on the beach, and so there was no doubt it would be one great week in our Army Air Corp career. We spent all day on the beach and most of the night out drinking and living it up.

All good things come to an end! When the good times ended that week, I was sent to Amarillo, Texas to be reassigned. I did not know whether it would be as a crew member on a B-29 or as an instructor on aircraft mechanics or gunnery school.

As it came to pass, my career in the Air Corp was about to come to an end. I had to take a complete physical exam, and I did not pass it due to my eighth auditory nerve being blown away from all of the noise and created by the 50 caliber machine guns firing in the B-17's, during our missions over Europe. I had really looked forward to something more to serve my country at this time, but it was not to be. I had actually wanted to make a career of the military, but at the end of November 1944, I was preparing to be transferred to Borden General Hospital in Chickasha, Oklahoma to start lip reading classes.

Before I left Texas, I received word that my wife had given birth to a little girl, but I could not get another furlough, because I had just been home the first part of that month.

I arrived at Borden general in early December and immediately started classes in lip reading. I found that I was not alone with this problem, but it did not make me feel any better. Right away, we were told that after completing these classes, we would be issued hearing aids and then discharged. I was caught with mixed emotions about his news. I definitely, wanted to

59

be back with my wife and baby, but I also wanted to continue serving my country and pursue my career in the military.

I know that I have led a wonderful life, even the thirty-five missions over Germany and enemy occupied France, Belgium and Holland, in which all ten of us survived. It was an honor to have served my country in this capacity.

On February 14, 1945, I was given an Honorable Medical Discharge and issued severance pay and was told that as of that moment, I was a Civilian again. I was warned of the possibility of being robbed before getting on the train because it had happened to others after they left the hospital. I knew that this was good advice, so when I got in town, the first thing I did was buy my ticket to Danville, Illinois. Then, I went to see a movie until time to catch the train. When I came out of the theatre, I had the **WILD URGE** to own a pair of cowboy boots. Why pass up the opportunity? I bought a pair and wore them on the train **HOME.**

A short time after the train left the station, a couple of M. P.'s came down the aisle and immediately saw me in uniform and the cowboy boots. One of them told me that he would have to report me for being out of uniform because those boots were not Government Issue. He asked to see my orders to be traveling. I just smiled at him and without saying a word, I just handed him my discharge papers. As he handed it back to me, all he could say was, "Damn, you have to be the luckiest ex G. I. In the world!"

I arrived home in Danville, Illinois late at night on February 14, 1945, Valentine's Day, to begin making adjustments back into being a civilian.

Helen had received a letter from the Government telling her that I would not be the same man that she knew that left for England upon my return to America. The letter tried to explain to her about effects that combat can have on G. I.'s, and that her patience and understanding would help me in adjusting back to civilian life. I shall never be able to thank God enough for giving me a wonderful understanding woman like Helen, who helped me in every way possible to adjust back into Civilian life.

As I had stated before, I had not completed high school, so I had several different jobs the first few years. I worked for my father-in-law at his gas station, the New York Central Railroad, drove a Pepsi Cola truck, Body and Fender work at a Chevrolet Dealership, then at a Pontiac Dealership, International Harvester Farm Equipments, and finally as a welder for Hyster Company, a lift truck builder.

After doing several welding jobs, I was called into the office and asked if I would be interested in a supervisor's position. I could hardly wait to get home to tell Helen the good news. I had always wanted to make a better living for my wife and daughter. After I had been a welding foreman for a couple of years, I decided to go back to school and get my G.E.D. The extra effort finally paid off; raises came more often and by the time that I thought about retirement at age 62, I had reached the classification of Technical Supervisor and was qualified to work in any department.

My retirement party was on September 30, 1986, and all of the Hyster Company employees attended for cake and coffee. Some of them probably to make sure I was REALLY leaving. Someone asked me where I was going to live after my retirement. I said, "I'm going to tie a snow shovel on the front of my car and drive until someone asks me what that thing is." I would know then that they never had to use one! Just joking of course.

Helen and I had our 50th wedding anniversary party on May 31, 1993, at a popular place called the "Beef House" over close to Covington, Indiana. We had our close family and about thirty-five friends with us to celebrate. It was an extremely enjoyable day. When the waitress brought the bill out, I told her to give it to the young man at the end of the table. It was my granddaughter's husband, Mike. I knew that he did not have any money, and he just about had a coronary when he saw how much it was. I walked over and took it from him and said, "What are you doing with this anyway?" Everyone got a big laugh from the expression on his face. I also said that fifty years ago when Helen and I married, "That night, she was crying, but tonight, **"I WAS CRYING!"** She was so cute and said, "Oh, I was not crying." She was embarrassed. We all laughed. I loved her so very much. She was a wonderful wife and mother. Both Sheila and I could always depend on her.

I have never been sorry about taking early retirement because my wife and I had eight good years before her death, suddenly on the morning of February 16, 1994. I felt as if my entire world had fallen apart. When I called my daughter, Sheila to tell her that her mother had just died, and then when I called my niece, Melanie, that her aunt had just passed away, it was one of the hardest things I have ever had to do. Sheila stayed two weeks with me, and then I told her it was time for me to take her home. I drove her to Douglasville, Georgia, and I returned HOME to an empty house, an empty bed. Everyday, I went to the cemetery and would sit at the grave and talk and cry. Everyone thought I was doing great. Little did they know just what it means to lose your spouse after fifty years of marriage. Everyone went home, and I was left to deal with the emptiness that I felt inside. I wished that it had been me instead of her, but of course, God was not finished with me. I still had lessons to learn. I also was yet to meet this beautiful Yellow Rose of Texas.

Difficult Days

Nine months after Helen's death, I made one of the biggest mistakes of my life. I want people to know how conniving some women can be, and that some will stop at nothing to get what they want. After a short period of steady dating, I married Mabel Holycross Estes from Danville, Illinois. She took her first husband's name, after she divorced a second husband whose name was Agan, a Pentecostal Minister. It seemed I was always running into her. I wonder now if she had run into me deliberately, as she had been divorced twice and I remember what she had said to Helen the few times we ran into her. She and Helen had gone to school together, and a few times when Helen and I were out and about, we ran into her, and Helen would say, "Why don't you get married?" She would always say, "Because I can't find a good husband like you have." Perhaps, when it came out in the paper about my Helen's death, she set her trap then. I will never know that for sure, but I married her, and she wanted to move to Florida where her daughter lived. This meant getting rid of my home, and Mabel got rid of all the furnishings. She also destroyed some of my memories that can never be replaced: documents and papers from the past that would be great in this book. I did love Florida because of the cold in Illinois. I loved Danville too, as my wife was buried there now, and also, I still have many friends there, but I have arthritis in my hands, and they are bent at the joints of my fingers. The cold really bothers me, so I was willing to move.

Mabel kept saying what good friends she and Helen had been growing up, but later on, she said that she had been through two divorces and never got anything from them, and she would see that I would have to TAKE CARE OF HER THE REST OF HER LIFE. She was never a good friend of Helen's growing up. If she had been, she would have continued to be Helen's friend after we married. Sheila, my daughter, had never met her even though we lived in the same town.

After moving to Florida, we went to lunch one day, and before we got to the restaurant on 17th street, I told Mabel that I had the worst headache that I had ever had in my life. We sat down to order, and I got sick at my stomach and went to the restroom. I threw up while in the restroom and then returned to the table. I got sick again and returned to the restroom where I threw up again. We ordered our meal, and I don't remember anything after that. Somehow, she got me to the car. I suppose with help from someone at the restaurant. She took me home and called her daughter. Her daughter came to the house and one of them called 911 for an ambulance that took me to the emergency at Doctor's hospital where Dr. Mayer was on call. To this day, I have wondered why she did not call 911 when we were at the restaurant. Perhaps, she wanted me to die then, and then reconsidered, as she had not acquired her an income. I did recover after the two brain surgeries and after rehabilitation. I am totally well today and recovered without being permanently crippled.

From the start, Mabel was insanely jealous, and she wanted me to have nothing to do with my daughter and her family. I was not even allowed to go to the barber shop alone, as she never trusted me and said that both of her prior husbands had run around on her. I really doubt that statement.

Even though Sheila's in-laws lived at Punta Gorda, and they would pass down I-75, she did not stop to see me, because Mabel made her feel unwelcome. She and Bill would later call from Punta Gorda and ask us to meet them at a restaurant near Punta Gorda, and we would drive down and have dinner with them.

My daughter and niece, Melanie did come to Sarasota to see me during the time I was in the hospital to visit me. After my daughter went back to Douglas County, Georgia, her home, she had a heart attack and a stroke, so I did not see her for almost five years. When she got well, she drove down to see me, and I hugged and kissed my little girl that had grown into a woman and gone through so very much grief, and had thought she would lose her father and her own life, but God helped us both to regain our health.

After Sheila left, Mabel, who had been in the hospital and had a bruise on her from the I-V, started screaming at me, and telling me that hugging and kissing my daughter was not appropriate actions for a man my age. She was wild with anger. I knew Mabel was jealous, but to accuse me of inappropriate actions toward my own daughter who had lost her only son one grandson, her mom and then to almost lose me and her own life was inexcusable. Mabel was clawing at my hands and arms with her nails, which were tough because she always went to have her nails done at one of the oriental places. I held her hands and told her to stop it. I thought I had her calmed down. We went to see a Dr. Harris, a doctor that I did know, and Mabel asked what she should say to the doctor, and I said to tell them the truth. When we got to the doctor's, she had called her daughter and told me that she was going in without me. She was in his office for a long time. I waited and waited, and then two police officers came into the office and on back to where the doctor, nurse, Mabel and her daughter were. The two officers came back out to where I was sitting and asked me to step out in the hall. After going with them, the one officer asked me if I had ever had my rights read to me. I said, "No, I have never had a reason for my rights to be read to me." He then said, "You have the right to remain silent, also you have the right to have legal representation, and anything you say, may be used against you in a court of law. I told him what had REALLY happened

And showed them my arm. Then, he went back into the inner office and a few minutes later came out and said that she admitted being the FIRST TO ATTACK. He then asked me if I wished to press charges against her. I said, "NO, that I didn't want anymore trouble," because I did not realize how far it would go and what she was planning. Then he said to sign this paper and go home. He said that Mabel would go home with her daughter and would contact me later. The next day she called and said we would have to talk about it. When I said we could meet for lunch; she said she would call later. A week went by before her son-in-law, Michael Burks, stopped by and told me that he had overheard her telling her daughter, Deborah Burks, that she was going to have me removed from MY OWN HOUSE. Later that night, two deputies came with an official injunction against me. I had ten or fifteen minutes to pack and get out of my home. Money from my pension check was missing from this envelope where I kept it when I cashed the check. There was $400.00 in the envelope before I took her to the doctor, so she had taken it, knowing what she was planning to do: to accuse me of abuse. I went to the ATM machine to get some money, as I had less than twenty dollars. A slip came out saying that the daily amount had been taken. I had no other recourse but to use my credit card to obtain money to leave Sarasota and drive to Douglasville, Georgia, where my daughter and son-in-law lived, as I did not have any relatives in Florida.

It was after midnight when I finally got on I-75 and headed North. One of the officers asked me if it would be alright if he prayed for me before I got on the highway. I thanked him and said he was only doing his job.

I called my daughter and told her what had happened. She was as upset as I was and told me to get a motel room for the night and come up the next day. I was too upset at that time, so I drove all night and arrived at her home the next morning at 9:30 AM.

When I got to Georgia, after a few days passed. I knew that I would have to get a divorce, as this jealousy and conniving had gone much too far, for way too long. My daughter, Sheila Gold, called someone and they gave her a phone number of Michael Moran's Law Firm. They made us an appointment to see Mr. Finebloom, and later on, Mr. Finebloom left the office of Michael Moran and sent me a letter to sign to keep him as my lawyer. I signed the letter, as he had been in the law office of Michael Moran, so I thought he would be alright, as he was the one Michael Moran turned me over to for him to handle my divorce. Later, I got a letter from Michael Moran, but I had already sent the letter retaining Mr. Finebloom.

Helen died instantly with a heart attack, and I was not equipped to know anything about divorce and how a man can be taken for everything he has and become homeless.

After she had me removed from our home, I stayed seven months with my daughter and her husband, because I did not have enough money to rent an apartment, nor did I have any furniture or anything, as Mabel kept everything. I don't know what she told the law. I signed and did not read anything. I really was not in any condition, as I was still recovering from two brain surgeries. I never dreamed someone could twist the law around like it was twisted around, and I feel like JUSTICE was not granted to me. I trusted the law, my lawyer, judges and everyone concerned. She uses my name, and I don't feel she is worthy to carry my name. She gets $500 a month alimony, almost all the proceeds from the sale of our place in Florida, and drug the divorce out, so that she also draws my Social Security. She did tell me one time that when her ex husband, Mr. Estes, died that she divorced that worked for the railroad that she would be able to draw benefits from him. He has died since our divorce, so she is drawing his railroad benefits. I feel the alimony should be stopped, or at least reduced by the amount of my Social Security she is drawing. She had no money when we married and brought nothing into the marriage. I worked at Hyster thirty years to get my pension and now, I have to pay $500 of the $700 to her called alimony. She could have worked thirty years the same as I did for a pension. It is not justice that she should be getting mine.

My lawyer was not acting in my best interest, or he would have said, "We will counter sue her, as she has admitted to initiating the attack", and it is on the Sheriff's papers.

I know now that my lawyer should have filed an injunction against her as she attacked me first, instead of letting her get away with making me sound like an abuser. I resent this more than anything. I guess that is what hurts the most is that she has smeared my GOOD NAME. With the court, she was able to make them think that my feelings for my only grown married daughter was not appropriate. My first wife died from a heart attack without any warning. I found her dead lying in our bed. Then Sheila thought she was going to lose her father when I had two brain surgeries. I think had I not hugged and kissed her, then that would have been inappropriate action, uncaring actions. My daughter and I lost three of the people in our lives that made the sun shine for us, and it had been almost five years since we had seen each other.

Sheila married Bill Gold, and he told me that when he needed to talk to someone, he could always call his mom and tell her whatever was bothering him, and it made him feel better to be able to do this. I have always loved Bill and he has been a fine son-in-law, and he has been good to my daughter and grandchildren and great grandchildren.

I feel that Bill probably loves my daughter more today than he did when they first married. He has been good to me as well. Especially, when I was homeless.

"When I became a Christian, Jesus forgave me of my sins, and I gave up the right to not forgive others no matter what terrible things they have done to me, especially Mabel." and I really don't want to judge her. I wish that I could forget as well as forgive, but forgetting will never be as I have to make out a check every month for $500 and mail to her. I still cannot believe the injustice that she was able to sway the courts. I signed everything under great stress. I know now that she never intended for us to get back together. It was a stormy relationship from the first, and I should never have married her in the first place. I was too lonely when we married and could not see the trees for the forest. She did almost destroy me, for I lost the will to live.

I don't know what I would have done without the love of my family. My daughter took me to the Senior Center in Douglasville, Georgia. She also took me to Martin's, a coffee shop where a group of men met every morning, and also to the American Legion where I met other Veterans and began playing Bingo, and made some very good friends at all three of those places.

When I married Melba, all of them were so very happy for the two of us, and they love her too. I know that to have a friend makes one wealthy, and we feel that we are millionaires because of the love of all these friends that we have both made in Georgia.

My granddaughter's husband, Mike Mallory married Melba and me at four in the afternoon on September 5, 2007, with my family and her son and his lady friend, and three of my men friends. One, David Prince, was my best man, Bob Jackson another friend sang "How Great Thou Are", and my friend, Frank Bellis took photos. Melba's youngest son, Dusty was there to give his mom to me, and his lady friend, Joyce Cooper, was Melba's maid of honor. After the short service, we all went to Logan's Roadhouse and all ate. I intended to feed all of us, but when I asked for the bill, the waitress said that it had been taken care of. Melba's son had paid the bill, and when I asked the waitress who paid the bill, she said, "The gentlemen at the end, and he said the groom should not have to pay for dinner."

Many times when Melba and I are out in public, people will ask about my experience in the military, and want to know what I did. When I say that I was a ball turret gunner hanging out of the bottom of a B-17, they want to hear some about the experience and how I felt. I can say that all of us went through World War II, trying to stay alive, keeping alert, so that we could fulfill our duty for our job in order to keep our crew alive, and praying that God would keep us all alive to return to see our unborn babies and our wives and family. No one can know this without having experienced the loneliness at night when one went to bed in a far away place, knowing the next mission could be your last. We had faith in each other as a crew and in our God that He would take us safely home, and He did just that. I know that a greater power rode with us on every mission, for without His presence aboard our B-17, we could not have made it back to America.

I was so devastated when Helen died. I felt that my world had been blown to bits, and even though my friends tried to help me, they could not. I never knew such grief.

I thought when I hired a lawyer who knew the law, that justice would prevail. I thought every American under our constitution was entitled to life, liberty and the pursuit of happiness. I am to blame for not reading what I signed, but this was my first experience at divorce and being homeless and having the law to come and tell me I had to get out. I was stunned beyond belief that this was happening to me. She knew she was guilty, for she had attached to the divorce papers that I would never try to have her put in jail for attacking me, and I signed it under my lawyer's advise. I know that I should have gone to the Sheriff's office myself and had her picked up for attacking me, but I was not raised to send a woman to jail. Am I doomed to live the rest of life with this woman always interfering in my life? I would like to get on with my life. Get her out of it forever, but every month, there is that check to write that takes from my income. I don't owe her this.

Her profession of faith is suspect, and the bible says everyone that says, "Lord, Lord, shall not enter the portals of Heaven."

She had not been a wife to me since the brain surgery. I knew that she was never going to be again, so I would say that our marriage actually ended in 1999.

On my way up I-75, the night the law told me that I had to leave my home, I decided that I had all I could stand of

Mabel's insane jealousy and false accusations, and when I returned to Sarasota, I would sue for divorce. After having such a wonderful life with my first wife, I just could not understand something like this.

Quite often, I catch myself wondering how many other VETERANS might be going through similar situations as this. I read a lot, and the little paper that comes out at Bay Pines Hospital is always talking about the homeless veterans, and I feel many in this state are homeless because of divorces such as mine in which the woman lied and took their money. It is hard to deal with; being taken for everything that you fought for and worked for by a GUILTY woman, lawyer and the judicial system that won't take the time to listen to the whole story. I had a statement prepared to present my case to the judge, but the lawyer that I had didn't even speak up for me. Her lawyer and the judge dictated the terms of the divorce and the lawyer that I paid to represent me didn't say anything in my behalf.

Mabel was never made to face me with her lies. She, her lawyer, her daughter, the judge, my lawyer got in a room in which I was not allowed to attend and came to an agreement and my lawyer would throw something at me and say, "Sign this". I didn't have any hearing aids at that time, so I missed out on about everything that was said. My lawyer finally advised me to sign the papers because there wasn't anything else he could do. I really didn't realize that I was signing away everything that I was entitled to. After the hearings were over, I was told that I could go into my home with the police officers and get everything that belonged to me. That was not to be. When I got there with my daughter and my niece, two police officers were there and they would not let me go in. Just the things that Mabel would let me have. She sat them out on the small enclosed room for Sheila and Melanie to carry out to my car. Now, I am told that too much time has gone by, and there isn't anything I can do, for I can not file abuse against her now. I had been ordered to pay $500.00 per month alimony besides the large amount of money that was given to her from the sale of the double wide manufactured home. It was my money that put twenty thousand dollars down when we bought the place in Florida. She didn't have any money, but she got most of it after the loan was paid off. All because a judge stated that I could afford to pay her five hundred dollars a month. She could have afforded to pay me, had she worked through the years as hard as I worked. This entire situation has left me feeling deeply hurt and bitter toward the judicial system of the state of Florida due to my legal rights being constantly denied!

Yes, I love my only child, my daughter. We have been to hell and back together with grief.

Remembering the old crew

I went through a lot during the war. At nineteen years of age, I was in England hanging out of the bottom of a B-17 as a ball turret gunner. If you think I was not scared, then think again. My wife was pregnant in the states and just sixteen. I loved my country and I loved this crew of men that fought with me for the freedom of America and the World. All are dead now except the radio operator and myself.

Whenever, I am near a B-17, I can feel their presence around me, and my memories go back in time to when we were all a crew depending on each other, and climbed aboard that beautiful FORTRESS knowing somehow in our hearts that God would bring us back after the encounter with the enemy. As I walk around that beautiful plane, I can see in my mind each of the members of the crew, and the position they filled while aboard that great FORTRESS. It sends cold chills up and down my spine. As people begin to ask me questions about what it was like and where different positions were located in the plane when we were on a mission. I find myself back in England in my mind with all the guys that made up our crew and the way each fulfilled their job. I loved them all. It was a feeling so deep that one cannot explain. For each mission, we were so close, depending on every man doing his job. We were a complete CREW of TEN MEN fighting for our lives.

Sometimes, I cannot talk about this or even think about it without the tears running down my cheeks. It is an experience indescribable in which God made young boys MEN, each depending on the other. Each of us knowing full well that he depended on his crew to do their part. I thank God that He allowed me the privilege to know and to love each of these men. It was a great experience. One that makes you respect life, liberty, love, loyalty, and all the many wonderful adjectives that built AMERICA.

I know that our forefathers felt this same way about this beautiful country called AMERICA.

We all loved her so much that we were willing to give our lives for her. No love is greater than the love of a man to be willing to lay down his life for his brother. That, my friends, is the type of people that AMERICA was filled with, not only in World War II, but from the beginning of her time.

After moving to Douglasville, Georgia, as I had no other place to go, my daughter seen to it that I would meet other people. She took me to the Senior Center where I started playing cards two days a week, and after renting an apartment, I would have coffee at Martin's, a place near the apartment every morning, to have coffee and sometimes biscuits and gravy. I met a lot of good people there who came in every morning. One man named David Prince, lived close by and had lost his wife a few years before. Earl Smith was also a regular customer, his wife was in a nursing home and later passed away. Copeland Jenkins and his wife Perline would come in on Wednesday and Thursday morning. He has three barber shops and would always be off those two days each week. Doyce Wood came in pretty regular when he wasn't driving cars for a dealership. Bob Jackson came in quite often when he wasn't working for the funeral home. All of these folks were good people and they became special friends.

I had also rejoined the American Legion and started going to the Senior Center to play Euchre. This is a mid western card game that most southern folks had never heard of.

One day, I talked David into going with me to the senior center to play Euchre. He was a retired police officer from Atlanta and like most other folks from that area, he had never heard of the game. He went with me and caught on to it real quick. From then on, he went every Tuesday and Thursday.

I began going to the American Legion every Sunday, Monday, Wednesday and Saturday night to play bingo and sometimes on Friday night for Karaoke. I really enjoyed the fellowship of the Veterans and I was made to feel welcome. Jim Stockton, an Iwo Jima survivor was a gunner in a tank group in the Marines. Frank Bellis had been a medic in the Navy during Viet Nam, and Joe Williams were the three that I developed a real close relationship with. Jim and I had so much in common because we had been gunners in very small spaces. He in a tank and I had been a ball Turret gunner in a B-17. We both agreed that we wouldn't have wanted the other ones job during World War II. Another good friend is Mark Koenig graduated as a Captain from West Point, and Sarge, my good friend, who is in the hospital with liver cancer.

Frank and I probably developed a stronger and lasting friendship, because we spent more time together. He was the one that encouraged me to start writing a book about my life. He made me feel special, because when I would walk in the club room, he would say, "There's my hero." I have tried to get him to write about his experience as a medic, but so far, he keeps saying there was nothing special to write about. I think he is far too humble, or he isn't ready to talk about it. Mark also calls me his "hero", and I don't feel like a hero, just their "special" friend.

I had stopped going to the senior center for some unexplained reason until one day, David said, "Why don't you come back and play Euchre today?" I didn't have anything to do that day, so I said, "I will meet you over there." Little did I know what God had in store for me that very afternoon, for in walked this tall dark haired blue eyed lady from Texas. She was a widow, and had recently moved there. She walked over and looked down at me, as I was seated, and said, "You do not look old enough to have been in World War II." There was an instant spark between us, and I thought to myself, "She is exactly what I have been searching for." I proceeded with caution for fear of being hurt again. Then I was told she was a widow, so somehow I knew that she had felt the same devastation that I had felt, and had gone through lonely times, much too lonely to be able to write about. She told me about sitting at the grave, crying, and I confessed to her that I had done this same exact thing with my beloved Helen. My friend David told me the next morning at coffee that that gal from Texas cannot keep her eyes off you. He was right. It didn't take us long to realize that we had fallen in love, and when I had returned from Colorado, and she was changing tables at the Euchre game at the senior center, I looked up at her and made my mouth into a kiss. To my surprise, she reached down and planted a very caring loving kiss on my lips, and my hat flew off. I said, "you have just made me flip my lid for you." I asked her if she wanted to go grab a bite to eat and go play Bingo with me. She said, "Yes," to my surprise. From that moment on, we have never been apart. We have bought a doublewide and moved here in late September to Sarasota, so that I can be near the doctors.

Shortly after I rented my apartment in Douglasville, I slumped to the floor just outside my door before going into my apartment where I would have been alone. The people across from me called the manager of the apartment who called 911 for an ambulance and then called Sheila, my daughter, who met me at the hospital. I stayed in the hospital several days, and they said that I had had a seizure, but another doctor told me it was caused from stress brought on by the divorce, being homeless, and having my teeth pulled and dentures put in, and that my system just could not take it, so you see, I was really in no shape to defend myself against any judicial system in a divorce or anything else. I had to trust my lawyer, but I know now that you cannot even trust your lawyer. I had to pay all the court cost, because I had filed for the divorce, but I had to get away from such an evil person.

After Melba and I got established in our new home in Sarasota, it was time to get re-established with the V.A. Hospital (Bay Pines at St Petersburg) I wanted to get new hearing aids and also new glasses.

The scheduling department made arrangements for me to get lab here in Sarasota at the VA clinic. The next morning after taking the tests, they called and sent me to the Doctor's hospital, as I needed 4 pints of blood. They did test to see where I was loosing blood. I was in the hospital four days due to my blood count being 6.9, and I was admitted to Doctor's hospital and given the 4 pints of blood immediately. When they did their test to see where I was loosing blood, they discovered that I had Barrett's esophagus. Since then, two times, I have had ablation therapy to burn out the Barrett's, which is a precancerous condition. The ablation therapy burns the Barrett's out, and I can live without the Barrett's. Also, I have Gerd, and will have to take Protonic the rest of my life. I feel this divorce and all the aggravation is what has made me ill. I also have a cancer on my leg that was cut out, but has returned, and will have an MRI next week and see the VA specialist here in Sarasota to see if it can be cut out again and gotten rid of permanently or if it will have to be treated with radiation.

I was born September 10, 1924, the last of the four Browning children. I was born in a railroad company house south of Danville, Vermillion County, Illinois. The son of Ralph and Mary Jenkins Browning, and for some unknown reason, given the name Elmer Eugene. I suppose to make an uncle feel good. Uncle Elmer and Aunt Mae lived just across the field from us at the time. My parents were divorced when I was small, and my mother told me that she did everything to get rid of me, to keep me from being born. She said, "You were stubborn and was born anyway." My sister, Merle, would say, "Oh, Mama, isn't he just the sweetest thing?" I know that it was a MIRACLE that I was born, and I am grateful to my God who still loves me and will someday, see that true justice shall come my way.

As I let my mind drift back to my childhood, the times that I thought were so bad, I know that now, that I have had time to reconsider where I am today, and where I came from; it really was part of the best time of my life. When I was five, my father married Florence Nelson, who had no children of her own. She was always very good to me, and I know that I was lucky to have had her for a mom, for it takes more than giving birth to be a real Mother. I will never forget this woman whom I believe loved me as any mother could ever love a son. Being raised by a step-mother and a father that truly loved all of the four small children that my father took custody of when he divorced my biological mother. My two older siblings actually were out on their own by the time that I was old enough to realize what life was all about. My older sister, Alice Lorene, was married at a very young age and when I joined the Army Air Corps at age eighteen, she had a little girl, Mary Melanie, who was almost two years old.

My brother, Robert, who was seven years older than me, left home just about two years after our father married Florence Nelson. I did not see him again until I was about to graduate from high school. I did not graduate from high school, but enlisted in the Army Air Corp. My other sister was two years ahead of me in school, and when she graduated, she left home, and it was many years before I saw her. My oldest sister left home shortly after our parents divorced, so I never really knew her until several years later.

My dad always wanted me to sing when we would go out to Florence's family, but to sing in school was another story. He also thought sports was unnecessary, and I loved both music and sports. I wish that I had been able to be a part of that when I was in high school.

Although Florence was only a step mother, she became the most loving mother that anyone could ever hope to have. I know that she loved my sister, Merle, and me as if we were her own. She and our father lived out their remaining years together. Florence died about three years after our Dad passed away. She was buried beside him in Sunset Cemetery north of Danville, Illinois. Although Florence never had any children, she became a true mother to Merle and me until the end of her life. She always tried to encourage us to be the best that we could possibly be in whatever we tried to do. Some of the things that I remember; she worked part time for a lady who lived in a small town about a mile south of our home. She never made much money, but she saved enough to buy me a new sled one Christmas. When I was twelve, the taverns in the city of Danville held a drawing every Friday night and gave the winner a hundred and twenty-five dollars. They pulled her name out, and the very next day, she took me to town and bought me a new bicycle at Montgomery Wards. On the way home, she stopped the car and said "I thought you might want to ride it the rest of the way!" As a proud owner of a new bike, that was the ultimate in loving thoughtfulness. I know that she was proud of me when I came home from overseas in full uniform with my medals and service ribbons and gunner wings on my chest. Helen and I went out to see my Dad and Florence said my dad was working. After hugging and kissing me with tears running down her cheeks, she said, "Why don't you go see your dad?" She told me where he was working that day, and as I started walking down the railroad track, one of my dad's friends saw me first and said, "There comes your son!" My dad turned to see me and came running to meet me. I know that my father loved me, and I, also, know that Florence, my step-mom, was a very special gift to me and our family. She loved me and my child and my grandchildren. At times, I miss her a lot and the talks we had.

One day, before I was old enough to leave home, I don't remember what I had done, but whatever it was, during one of our many conversations, Florence suddenly said, "Gene, the way you do things, I believe you will live to be a hundred and fifty and turn into a grindstone." I really don't know if that will happen or not, but I still have to smile every time I think about it.

My father was a section gang worker on the New York Central railroad, but we were still poor. It seemed as though everyone was leaving, and I grew up thinking that was the way it was supposed to be. In the middle of my seventeenth year, I left home and worked in a factory until I was eighteen. At that time, I must have been over flowing with patriotism due to "World War II" going full swing, so I enlisted in the Army Air Corp.

When I left school, I moved into town and stayed with Lorene and Melanie, and I found a job working for Allith-prouty Corporation until joining the military. We had a lot of government contracts.

To have had Florence to marry my father and take on the responsibility of four children was also something very wonderful, for how many step moms love their step children as they would love their own. I know that she loved me, and I was happy and trusted her.

I remember the first time my father brought her home. He had been courting her for awhile. We were not aware of this courtship. When they got married, he brought her to our house, and told us, "I have a surprise for you kids." Go to the bedroom and see what I have brought home. We only had one kerosene lamp, so it was dark when I walked into my father's bedroom. Florence reached out and touched my arm, as I came near their bed. It almost scared me to death, as I did not know what to expect, and could not see her in the darkness. There had not been a woman in our house, as my mother had left long before I could remember and my sister, Merle and my brother, Bob, and I were left to fend for ourselves whenever our father was working or courting Florence. Bob was always left in charge being the older one of the three. At the time, I thought that I had a tough childhood, but as I look back, I think how wonderful it really was, especially, for my father to have found such a wonderful woman, as OUR Florence. No mother could have been better to us, And no mother could have been better to me. It has helped to make me thankful for what I am today.

The next day and for several years afterward, I realized what a wonderful mother she had become to me. I will always remember her as a mother and a grandmother to my daughter and a great grandmother to my great grandchildren.

Sometimes, I look at the picture of my grandson, my only grandson, John David Gold, and I see that he looked like me when I was seventeen.

Although, Florence and my father lie in an unmarked grave north of Danville, I remember it as hallowed ground from two people of my past that I loved so much.

I feel that they were so important in making my life what it is today. I remember the talks that Florence and I had, and I know that she loved me as her own son, and I am very grateful that my father found such a wonderful woman to share our lives.

She was crazy about my grandson and my granddaughter, Gina, however, she never met Margaret, as she died before she was born.

My only daughter, Sheila, remembers her as the doting grandmother that loved her and her children. Her memories are all good of this wonderful grandmother who made her dresses when she was little. When she speaks of Florence, her eyes light up and she remembers her as a very loving person.

My life, like many other people's life, has been filled with much love, and also a lot of grief, but someday, God will take us all home, and there will be no more grief, and no more sadness. I only know that this has been a wonderful JOURNEY for me.

My first experience in tragedy was when my oldest sister was murdered by her estranged husband in her apartment in the city of Aurora, Illinois. My wife and I were watching the ten o'clock news on channel three when the reporter came on with the story. Needless to say, this is an extremely shocking way to be notified of a death of a sister that you had loved all the many years. She was survived by a young teenaged daughter. My wife and I made plans to drive up to Aurora and bring Melanie to our home to make sure she had a loving family to live with. We wanted to comfort and console her during this difficult time of her grief. This was indeed a trying time in our lives.

We later had to put her in a foster home, as she was accustomed to just doing as she pleased, and we were raising our own daughter, and it created a lot of friction. It was one of the hardest things Helen and I ever had to do. I wish it had worked out, for both Helen and I felt she needed to be with her family. Perhaps, if she had lead a structured life style, we could have kept her in our home with us. When she lived with her mother and Alexander, he did not want her around, and when she came home late, he would not let her inside the house and would make her sleep on the steps, and often times, when this happened, she could only get food from the trash. I did not know all this had taken place, and when Alexander murdered her mother, I just knew that I wanted her with us. She was already a teenager by then and I was unaware that no one cared where she went, and she did as she pleased, which we all know that the teenage years are rough, and are only worse when no one seems to care where you go or what you do. We had rules that Sheila, our daughter, had to live by, and these same rules applied to Melanie, but she would not adhere to them. In later years, she realized that we had truly tried to do our best for her, and she is now in her 60's, and she knows that I love her a lot.

The Chicago Sunday Tribune, January 6, 1957 had the following head lines:

SEIZE HUSBAND IN ATTEMPT
TO STRANGLE WIFE
Find Aurora Woman in Critical Condition

An Aurora husband, seized as a fugitive near Watertown, Wisconsin, Friday night when his auto crashed into a truck, agreed to waive extradition yesterday on an assault to murder charge in the attempted strangulation of his estranged wife. Mrs. Alice Voskuil, 35, found unconscious, with a silk stocking knotted around her neck, in her room at 18 S. Root St., Aurora, was in St. Charles hospital there in critical condition from a cerebral blood clot.

Held in Jail

Her husband, Alexander, 38, of 221 S. Lake St., Aurora, held in the Dodge county jail in Juneau, Wis., admitted to Sheriff Ed Kleeman that he beat and choked her. He will be returned to Aurora after a court hearing tomorrow. Mrs. Voskull was found by her landlady, Mrs. Myrty Mason. Unable to tie the knot, Mrs. Mason cut the stocking with scissors and summoned help. The landlady also told of seeing Voskull drive away a short time before. An Illinois radio alarm for Voskull was broadcast to Wisconsin Friday evening. Twelve minutes later, Voskull was captured when his auto collided with a truck seven miles north of Watertown. Voskull was injured slightly.

Separated Since March

Voskull, an employe of the Lindsay Chemical company in West Chicago, said he and his wife had been separated since last March. He said he received a phone call Friday that she was seeing a man with whom she had been friendly prior to her marriage to Voskull. Mrs. Nadeen Stele, R.F.D.4, Fox River Heights, acknowledged making the phone call. She told police that her husband, Everett, had been going out again with Mrs. Voskull.

The paper for June 27, 1957:

VOSKUIL GETS 90 YEARS
Sentenced After Pleading Guilty

Wife Killer given Lengthy Term by Judge Seidel,
Eligible for Parole in 30 years.

Alexander Voskuil, 40, formerly of 221 S. Lake St., Aurora, *was sentenced to serve 90 years in the Illinois State Penitentiary at Joliet Voskuil had pleaded guilty to the murder of his wife, Alice, whom on Jan. 4, he had assaulted and tied a silk stocking tightly around her neck. She died on Jan. 7 at St. Charles hospital without regaining consciousness.*

It had snowed the day before, and the day of the funeral, the wind was blowing and picked up part of the snow, and it would become snowballs and roll down the hill. The wind would keep them rolling and by the time they quit rolling, they were the size of basketballs. I had never seen this before nor have I ever seen it since. When Melanie came in January to visit Melba and Me, we talked about how very strange it was to see this.

Melanie went on to graduate from high school with scholarships to the University of Denver. Later on, she went to nursing school and after graduating, worked for a doctor for awhile and then for a hospital. Her husband, Ray, worked for IBM for twenty-five years in Topeka, Kansas. They raised three children, Leslie, Eric and Allan before moving back to Colorado, Ray's home state. They have a beautiful home east of the Rocky Mountains in Longmont. When I was out visiting, it was so enjoyable to take my coffee out on the patio and sit in the swing and gaze at the snow capped mountains over to the west. The weather was really warm the few days that I spent in Colorado but there was a nice breeze that was always present as I sat in the swing enjoying my morning coffee and the beautiful Rocky Mountains. I am very proud of her, and I know that she thinks of me as the only father that she ever knew.

I am so thankful that Florence lived to hold two of my daughters, Sheila's, children on her lap. She loved them and said she was so happy to have a granddaughter and two wonderful great grand kids. She often bragged about Gina and John being such beautiful and good kids. It is a shame that she never lived long enough to know Margaret, the youngest daughter of Bill and Sheila's. Margaret has a beautiful little daughter, Isabella called "Bella" for short.

Gina and Mike have a nice family Josh, who enlisted in the Air Force and left for basic September 11, 2007. I am so proud of him for wanting to serve his country. Sarah and Jake are both in high school and very active in band in Douglas County, Georgia.

My only grandson, John David Gold, was accidentally shot by his best friend while cleaning their guns in the home of his friend and family. This was a second tragedy that we had experienced in our family. Everyone has to deal with situations such as this in their own way. Besides, my own grief, I had to be strong for my wife and family. You never get over the part of missing one that you love and the feelings of the mother and father of their only son, two sisters of the lost sibling and two grandmothers, my wife, who had developed a love so strong for these three grand children. I know that my wife never got over the loss of John David, and I really feel that it was a part of the reason for her early demise. She was unable to feel comfortable going into Sheila's house again, and we always got a motel room in Douglasville, after that, whenever we came down to visit. She did tell Sheila why she could not stay at their home anymore. Bill, the father of John David, upon our arrival in Georgia, was a man trying so hard to hold himself together for his family, but I saw him go into another room, and ram his fist through the wall. John David was cremated, his memorial was held at the high school where he attended, and I never saw so many people, hundreds of students, families and friends came to try to console my daughter and her husband and the family. Today, Bill works very hard, many hours. I also know that none of us will ever forget this handsome young man that brought so much joy into our lives during his short life. I also know that someday, we shall all meet again in a place where we shall never have to say "goodbye".

John David, the last time that I had been with him, had taken me to Wal-Mart and showed me a Winchester rifle, and told me that was what he wanted when he graduated from high school, which was coming up that year. I told him if that is what you want, that is what you will get, but he never lived that long. A clerk was standing there, and I said, "Unlock the case and let John hold the gun." Then I told him to lock it back up and keep it, for we will come back to get it for his graduation but it was not meant to be. He had taken me there to show me the Winchester, as he thought it was so very beautiful.

When we received the phone call from Bill, our son-in-law, Helen could do nothing but sit and scream until I finally went to our medicine cabinet and got a valium and a glass of water. After we both calmed down a little, we started packing to get ready for our drive down to Georgia. This was without a doubt the hardest trip we ever had to make. When we walked into their kitchen, Sheila's friend, Caroline was standing by the sink, and she said that Sheila had just told her, "My Daddy will be here pretty soon, and everything will be alright." I knew that there was no way I could make it alright. I also knew that I had to be strong for my family. I tried to be calm on the outside, but deep down inside of me, I was being crushed and torn apart. I just could not believe our only grandson was gone. To this very day, I don't know how our only daughter and son-in-law were able to keep their sanity. I truly believe that this was a contributing factor to my wife passing away at such an early age. She was only 68 when she passed away. The doctor in the emergency room told me that if he had been there at the time, he could not have saved her. We had just finished eating breakfast, and she told me that she did not feel well and was going to lie down. She went to the bedroom and later, I went in to check on her, and found her dead. I called 911, and the ambulance took her to the hospital.

Gina was pregnant with her first son, Joshua when her brother John was shot, so there is no way to describe the agony and sorrow that she was living with at that time. About a year later, she and her husband were divorced. She moved with her baby back home with her mother and father. Several months later, she and a girl friend shared an apartment in Douglasville. Some time, later, she met and fell in love with a young guitar player, Mike Mallory. He was playing with a small group that played country music. Their first son, David, was just three months old when he was a victim of S.I.D.'s. Another tragedy of which we are never ready. We had been down to Douglasville for a visit and the day after we had arrived back home, we received a call from Margaret telling us that David had died. Once again, we packed our luggage and made another sad trip to Georgia.

Mike and Gina had a new home built back in the woods behind Bill And Sheila's house. There they began raising their children Josh, Sarah, and Jake.

Besides working full time as a sheet metal worker, Mike has become an ordained minister of the gospel.

On February 12, 1943, I found myself at Scott Field, Illinois, and immediately started wondering "What in the world am I doing here"? I'll skip the boring part of basic training and aircraft mechanic school and gunnery school.

The girl that I had been dating when I enlisted came down to Gulfport, Mississippi. We were married on May 31, 1943. She was sixteen and I was eighteen, just a couple of dumb kids that had no idea of what we were doing. We did love each other, and that love grew and survived for us for over fifty years.

As I write this story, my thoughts go back to the happy times in the past. There were all of the good years with my loving wife, Helen, and our beautiful daughter Sheila, who was born on Thanksgiving day 1944, and I was unable to take another leave, as I had just returned to Oklahoma to the base, so Helen went through this pregnancy and the birth of our only child alone except for one fifteen day furlough. It seems only yesterday that our little girl grew up into a lovely lady, married a terrific fellow, Bill Gold, and the two of them started a family of their own. First, a daughter, Gina, then a son, John, and then another daughter, Margaret.

Life was so good for my family. Everyday, we gave thanks to our God in Heaven for the many Blessings that He had given. One day, Bill and Sheila came to our home and said that the company that he worked for had offered him a promotion, but he would have to move from Danville, Illinois, to Atlanta, Georgia. After considerable thought, they decided to take the offer and started making plans to make the big move. Time passed much too swiftly, and our grand children grew up to be wonderful young adults. Gina was married and John and Margaret was in high school in Douglasville, Georgia.

On the morning of February 2, 2008, Melba and I were watching the news, and the announcer started telling about a B-17 that had come to the Venice Airport. It was going to be there for four days and would let people take walk through tours. We had just finished breakfast and was trying to decide what we wanted to do that day. When this story came on the

TV, Melba said, "Let's get our shower an get dressed and drive down there." I am so glad that she enjoys seeing this beautiful aircraft as much as I do. Having been on a bomber crew during World War II, and flying all of my missions over Germany, I still get a terrific thrill out of being close to one of them again and again. I guess that I will never get tired of seeing these wonderful B-17's as long as I live. Being a part of the best crew of ten that ever flew these planes, it brings back wonderful memories of the times that we spent together.

Everytime I get close to a B-17, I can almost feel the presence of the other nine young men that had been molded into a combat crew.

As we walked around this plane that Saturday, several people would stop us; seeing my WWII cap, that I wear all the time, and they asked me questions about the plane and what it was like being a ball turret gunner flying over Germany in combat.

This is the fourth time in the past few years that I have had the opportunity to get close to one of these planes from the past. Each time, there are others there that have had the experience and opportunity to spend time in their past with a combat crew.

This particular day was no exception. We met a man that had been a radio operator with a crew based in England.

Like me, he and one other member of his crew was all that was left.

As we walked around the right wing of that plane Saturday afternoon, we came face to face with a fellow that had also been a ball turret gunner and had been with the 97th bomb group that was just a few miles from the 401st bomb group that I had been with.

He told us that their plane had been shot up pretty bad and his pilot had to ditch it in the North Sea just a short distance from the German Coast. They all got out of the plane and into their rubber life rafts before it slowly sank to the bottom of the sea. It was really sad, hearing him tell of being picked out of the water by the Germans and taking them to stalag four prison camp, where he spent the rest of the war. As he told how his memory had faded, by being a prisoner of war, I could not resist the urge, and I gently put my arms around his shoulders and gave him a big hug. I didn't even get his name, but I'll always remember his face as we parted and slowly walked away. Each time that I meet someone like this, I have to thank the Lord for the many blessings that he has given me.

I will always be grateful that God found a useful job for me, that of defending my country in its hour of need. I still believe in this country, and someday, someone will help me to find Justice.

Maybe, because of my advanced age, I can't help but let my mind wander back over the years. When our crew went to Dyersburg, Tennessee after being formed in Salt Lake City, my wife, Helen, came down from Danville, Illinois to spend as much time with me as we were allowed to have. We had a room in downtown about twelve miles from the Air Base, and I was permitted to live there as long as I was off duty. We were on a pretty demanding training schedule as a complete crew before leaving the United States. Needless to say, we really cherished every minute that we could spend together. This was the first three months of 1944, and we were pretty sure that when our first anniversary came the last day of May, that we would be half the country and an ocean apart. Not knowing weather we would ever see each other again.

After talking about it at great length, we decided that we would not plan a family until I came home from overseas. The last evening before we were to ship out from that Air Base, we were all called to the Post Theatre for our final instructions. At this time, we were told that the next morning, we would go by train to Kearney, Nebraska where we would be assigned a brand new B-17G that still had the assembly line smell on it. My heart really sank to a new low. Thinking I might never see my young wife again, because the last words from the officer in charge, were "You are all restricted to the base and no passes will be issued tonight."

With a heavy heart, I walked out of the theatre, and to my surprise, there stood my wife with two other wives of a couple of guys that were from a different crew. I was so happy to see her, but I had to know how they had managed to get on the base.

She said that they had heard that we were leaving the next morning, so they caught a ride with an officer that was coming out from town. He told all three of them that he would sign them in as officer's wives. Where there is a will, there is a way. Right away, she said that she would catch a bus the next morning and go home , so she could pack some clothes and get a train ticket to Kearney. I told her not to do it, because we wouldn't be there but just a couple of days. She had made up her mind so nothing I could say would stop her. Anyway, the morning before we went out to our plane, I had taken time to write her a short letter and left it with a friend in another crew that wouldn't be leaving for a few days. As it happened, the train that Helen was riding on heading west arrived in Kearney at midnight, and we had already landed at an Air Base in Manchester, New Hampshire, and was bedded down for the night.

Two days later, we once again loaded our gear aboard that beautiful aircraft and left our beloved country. Our route to the 401st Bomb Group was covered earlier in this story, so it took several weeks before any mail started catching up with us. After several letters, there came this one; in part, it said, "Our plans were wasted. I came home from Kearney pregnant!" What a shock! But, of course, I wrote back and said, "I didn't see you in Kearney." I had left a note, but I didn't think my pencil had been that powerful. The next letter explained that she had meant to say it happened in Dyersburg that last night before I shipped out. Of course, I remembered that I had kind of got carried away with my love making that night. Even to this day, I always say that it is no wonder that Sheila loves Georgia so much because she was conceived in the south, so that makes us Southerners by choice.

I had spent six weeks basic training in St. Petersburg, Florida where the drill sergeant really had his job cut out for him teaching a bunch of green recruits to be battle ready soldiers. When I enlisted into the Army Air Corp, back in February of 1943, I felt pretty strong that I did not want to be a foot soldier. After taking aptitude tests and completing basic training, some higher power decided to send me to Gulfport, Mississippi to start aircraft mechanic school. This was a five month period that lasted from April on into August and by the time it was over, I felt as if I had been dragged uphill. We were assigned classes from eleven at night to six 'clock in the morning. After an hour of calisthenics, we would have other duties to perform before we were allowed to go to bed. This being the hottest part of the day, it was extremely hard to sleep.

After graduating this school, I was walking by the bulletin board, and saw a notice that volunteers for gunnery school were needed. Right away, I decided that was what I had wanted to be.

September 15, 1943, I was in Kingman, Arizona and started classes on how to become an aerial gunner. These classes were a lot more interesting than the mechanic school. Besides, our regular classroom sessions, we spent time out on the gunnery range where we became familiar with fifty caliber machine guns and the operation of my future gunnery position, the ball turret.

95

We spent one week, just one hour each day detail strip-ping and then reassembling a fifty caliber machine gun. The instructor told us that by Friday, we would be required to do this blind folded.

Sure enough, when we went into our position on Friday, blindfolds in place, I started removing all of the screws and springs and placing each small part in a box, so that I could reverse the procedure after having the gun completely apart. When I told the instructor that I was ready to reassemble, he picked up the box and I could hear him shaking it to mix all of the small parts, so that I would have to identify each piece as I picked it up. I found that he had put a broken piece and one bent one in the box. I was surely happy that I had paid close attention all week. As it happened that day, I completed my assignment second in the class of twenty-five individuals.

When we arrived in England and had to put our guns to-gether in the dark and set our solenoids by sound and touch, I really appreciated the training that we had in gunnery school back in Kingman, Arizona. The instructors we had back there were the very best.

As we get older, it is only natural that we start thinking about the friends we have had in past years. My case is no exception; since leaving my old home town in Illinois, I have learned that some of my best friends have since passed away. It was hard for me to believe that, to mention a few Axel Nelson, Jim Mariage, and Norm Divan. I'm sure there are others that I haven't heard about.

I am happy to say that there are some that I have been able to stay in contact with Don Longer and Jim Chittick are two that will always be held close as true friends. After making a couple of phone calls to Don, he in turn gave my phone num-ber to Jim and since then, he has made it possible to let me get in touch with Bob Ruch and Mike Allen. These men are some of the really good friends that have retired from Hyster company in Danville, Illinois. It has been quite a joy to talk to them on the phone and to hear that they are all doing well since joining the retirement ranks.

I had asked Jim Chittick if he would mail me a Cubs schedule, and today, I got the schedule and with it came a Cubs t-shirt, so that tells you what wonderful men I worked with at Hyster.

I know that my life has been filled with so very many wonderful friends, and I am most grateful to my God for these wonderful gifts.

I'm sure that Jim will be putting me in contact with others now that he has my phone number. There are several others who were in the same group that worked together during that period of time and since retired. Many I want to thank for helping me to do my job at Hyster, for with my hearing loss, when my name came over the loud speaker, someone had to tell me, for I would not hear it. These men helped me to overcome the hearing difficulty caused by riding in the ball turret directly behind the bomb bay, and the roar of the engines and sounds of the fifty caliber machine guns, as we shot at the German planes, and they also shot at us.

From the time I met Melba, I loved her, and I know she loved me too. We have so many things in common, and since the phone conversation with friends of mine from the past, she made a suggestion that perhaps, we could plan a trip up to my old hometown. Of course, it would have to be in the spring when the weather would be just an awful lot more to our liking than in the winter with all the snow and cold wind blowing. It would be pretty nice, seeing some of the "old folks". I know that she would enjoy meeting people that

I had worked with and other folks that I knew when I lived in Danville.

We have talked about taking a trip out through parts of Texas where Melba spent several of her years growing up and living, as well as going back up to Douglasville, Georgia, to visit good friends that we had met when we lived there before getting married and moving to Florida.

The reason we moved to Florida was because this is where I lived when I had the two brain surgeries, and I was having some pain in the back of my head, and Melba wanted me to come back here to go to Dr Mayer, the brain surgeon, as she felt he knew what he had done, and would be the best qualified to test me. We got into to see him, and they did test, and he said that my brain was alright.

While here, I brought Melba out to The Winds of St. Armon, and we purchased the doublewide and packed our belongings to make the move to our new home. Melba's son, Dusty, drove the U-Haul, and hired two Mexicans to load the truck. We followed him in my old Buick, and she in her Mercedes that we had loaded with clothing. Enroute Melba had called Kelli, the young lady that took care of the purchase of this doublewide. Kelli assured her that she would have two men the next morning come to unload the truck. They lived here, and even hooked up our washer and dryer. Everything was hauled in, and the boxes sat in the living room until we could unload them a few at a time. Dusty stayed two days, and we took him over to Bradenton to the pier that stretches out into the Gulf where one can fish and also a restaurant is there. We all enjoyed the food, and the wonderful warm Gulf. We took Dusty to the airport where he flew into the Atlanta airport, as Douglasville is just west of the Atlanta airport. I don't know what we would have done without his help. He is a wonderful son, both to me and to Melba. Later, he and Joyce flew to Orlando for a convention, and then rented a car to drive to Sarasota from there to pick up Melba's Mercedez that she had sold to him. We had traded in my old Buick Road Master for a beautiful Mercury Grand Marquie. We only have the one automobile, as that is all we need. We go everywhere together, and from the time she first asked me if I would like to spend the night with her, we have been together ever since.

After moving to Florida, I started getting re-established with Bay Pines VA hospital, and they set up a lab test for me at the Sarasota Clinic. The next morning after the blood test, they called and told me to go to the emergency room at Doctor's hospital, as my blood count was 6.9. They admitted to the hospital and gave me a half gallon of blood. They did test to see where I was loosing the blood. Since then, they have done several endscopies, and used a light to burn out my Barrett's, as it was precancerous. They will do this procedure one more time, the latter part of March 2008. While I was in the hospital, Melba only left for about an hour to come home and get some clothes and toilet articles, and then, she did not leave the hospital until she brought me home. We have never spent one night apart, and I have never known a woman who loves me the way she does. Perhaps, one has to lose a spouse to the grim reaper to know just how really wonderful it is to find love again. We know that we are two of the lucky ones. We don't want to be apart.

When I think about my life back in Danville, Illinois, my thoughts go to a group of people who were involved in several stage productions and performed in the Palace theatre on Vermillion Street. This organization was called "The Red Mask Players." Some well known people that got their start in their acting careers were Dick and Jerry Van Dyke and Gene Hackman. The grand lady that made it all possible was Kathryn Randolph, and she directed a great number of stage plays during her life.

I was a welder at Hyster Company when Betty Sue Kreidler came to our home and said that a new play was going to be cast, and she thought that I should come and take a part that was just right for me. I told her that I had never done any acting before, but she insisted in me showing up for a reading. The name of the play was "See How They Run", and it was a comedy which took place in England. She said that I had spent time in England and had the perfect cockney accent for the part of Sergeant Towers.

Red Mask Players

When my wife joined forces with Betty Sue, I finally agreed to give it a try. There were several people that had been in other plays, and I was a new comer. I was really nervous until I really put myself into the part. We practiced for several weeks and finally, it was time for opening night. By this time, I had become the character that I practiced to be. I was not nervous at all, but my wife, Helen, was so upset that she had to call our family doctor to get something to calm her down. She was in the audience and was afraid that I would forget my lines.

The play was a huge success and at the end, we made our curtain calls. I was so happy when only one other in the cast of eight performers had more curtain calls than me. As I started to leave the theatre, a small boy stopped me and held out his program and asked for my autograph. Naturally, I signed it Sergeant Towers.

Donald O'Conner also got his start in Danville, Illinois and Bobby Short was before my time, and I never met him, so I do not know how he got his start, but he was also from Danville, Illinois.

The next day when I went to work, the plant manager came out of the office and told me he had seen the performance, and

I was very good! I, jokingly said that after the review I had gotten, it was quite possible that I would head out to Hollywood and follow the footsteps of the two Van Dyke brothers and Gene Hackman. Just kidding of course, and then I thanked him for his kind words and told him that I would rather stay with Hyster Company and try to advance to a higher paying job and make a good living for my family.

I knew that there was no way I could ever be a success in the entertainment world. There were several stage productions after that, but I did not have any desire to try out for anymore.

My decision to stay with that job really worked out very well because I did receive several promotions and worked until I was sixty-two and then retired to a pretty decent life and not a worry in the world. My wife, Helen, lived for eight years, and we got to celebrate our fiftieth anniversary with our family and several friends.

I just glanced at the calendar a few minutes ago, February 12, 2008. This brings back memories of sixty-five years ago on this date, when I was sworn into the old Army Air Corp. It was midnight on the night of February 11, 1943 when I climbed on board a passenger train with a few other boys about my age going to Peoria, Illinois. Some of them had been drafted and two of us had joined because we knew that it would just be a matter of time before our number would come up. I have never regretted the day that I decided to join the Air Corp. I was over whelmed with a lot of patriotism and served with pride.

I AM STILL PROUD TO BE AN AMERICAN AND PROUD FOR THE OPPORTUNITY TO HAVE SERVED MY COUNTRY, FOR THIS IS TRULY THE GREATEST LAND IN THE WORLD.

LUCK OR MIRACLE

1. My mother said that she did everything possible to keep me from being born, but she said, "You were stubborn and was born anyway." This I consider to be a miracle that I was born.

2. When I was five, my father married Florence Nelson, who had no children. He had divorced my mother, Mary Jenkins, for adultery and got custody of all of his children. I believe this to be a miracle that Florence Nelson became my mother, not just a step mother, for she loved me dearly, and I loved her.

3. May 31, 1944, I married my sweetheart, Helen DeVore, she was sixteen and I was eighteen, It was a miracle that God put me with this wonderful young girl that became a lady with great conviction, and my wife for the rest of her life. With her help, I adapted back into Civilian life after 35 missions over Germany and enemy occupied countries, leaving America as a boy, and returning a man. It was difficult, but she was always at my side.

4. November 1944, our only child, a daughter, Sheila was born. This was our miracle child.

5. As a complete crew of ten, we flew thirty-five missions over Germany and enemy occupied France, Belgium and Holland. The entire crew of ten came through without a fatality.

Although it took seven B-17's to complete all the missions, I ask you "Luck or Miracle"

6. May 4, 1944, our target Berlin. The ball turret is one of the loneliest places in the plane; hanging out of the belly of a big bomber with the roar of four big engines lulling you into thoughts of the past and the future; if there will be any after this day. Without any warning, the weather started closing in, and I began hearing the most beautiful harp music that I had ever heard. I don't know how long it lasted, but all at once, our radio operator got the message from 8th Air Force control to scrub the mission and hit our secondary target. That very instant, the harp music stopped, and I never heard it again. "Luck or Miracle"

7. July 7, 1944, Target Leipzig. One blast directly under my turret blew out my fourteen inch sight window and a piece of shrapnel lodged right by my head, barely missing my head. "Luck or Miracle"

8. July 31, 1944, Target Munich. Every engine we had was hit, and our pilot brought us back to England and landed on an expanded metal runway. "Luck or Miracle"

9. Back in Civilian life, several years later, I was working as a supervisor in a lift truck factory in Danville, Illinois. One day right after lunch, as I walked toward my stand up desk, suddenly my eyesight failed and everything started spinning. I dropped down on my knees to keep from passing out. About that time, an office worker came by and asked me what was wrong. He helped me up to the office and the plant nurse called Medix. When I arrived at the hospital emergency, the doctors could not figure out what was wrong. Finally, after several blood counts, they rushed me into the Operating room, put me to sleep and cut me open to find that my appendix had burst. Ten days later and a drain tube installed, I went home. The doctor told me later that if a few hours had gone by before

they opened me, there was no way I could have been saved. "Luck or Miracle"

10. My wife, Helen De Vore, helped me to adjust back to civilian life after those 35 missions and the loss of my hearing. Without her undying love for me, she helped me to come back from the stress of everyday life as a ball turret gunner where I never knew if we would be one of the B-17's shot out of the sky "Luck or Miracle"

11. One mission, my hatch came open and I was almost sucked out of the ball turret. About half of the hatch opening was still open to the inside of the plane, and the radio operator had told me to put on my safety belt before returning to the ball turret to clear out my ammunition, but I was in a hurry and forgot The radio operator pulled, as I felt I was being sucked away through the opening. All at once, I felt a giant hand on my buttocks shoving me back into the plane, so I ask you? "Luck or Miracle"

12. On January 7, 1999, my wife and I went to lunch. I told her that I had the worst headache that I had every had. Instead of taking me to the hospital or calling an ambulance, Mabel drove me home and called her daughter, Deborah, who came to the house and told her to call an ambulance. Time had stopped for me. I don't remember anything until well after the first brain surgery. I lost control of my right arm and hand, and when the surgeon came into my room, and asked how I was doing, I told him I had lost control of my right arm and hand. He immediately took me back for a second surgery. Dr. Peter Mayer was on duty in emergency when the ambulance arrived with me. I know that God had guided his hands during the procedure once again "Luck or Miracle"

13. My daughter and niece did come to Sarasota to see me during this time to visit at the hospital. After my daughter went

back to Douglas County, Georgia, her home, she had a heart attack and a stroke, so I did not see her for almost five years. When she got well, she drove down to see me, and I hugged and kissed my little girl that had grown into a woman and gone through so very much grief, and she thought she was going to lose her father. God helped us both to regain our health, so? "Luck or Miracle"

14. On September 5, 2007, I married a beautiful tall dark haired, blue eyed lady whose husband had died after four and half years of fighting cancer. She had just moved to Douglasville, Georgia to be near her son. We moved to Sarasota to be near Dr. Mayer, and after moving here, I got reinstated with the VA Hospital, and they set up a lab appointment at the Sarasota clinic. The next morning, the doctor's nurse called and told me to go immediately to Doctor's hospital, as my blood count was down to 6.9. I was admitted to the hospital and given 4 pints of blood, and they did test to see where I was loosing blood. The endoscopy showed I had pre cancer called Barrett's Esophagus, and the doctor removed the Barretts. I would have bled to death, slowly had I not had that lab, and possibly died from cancer of the esophagus had the endoscopy not been done, so I ask you once again "Luck or Miracle"

15. MIRACLE - THE FUTURE. I know it will take a miracle for this nightmare of the divorce from Mabel to ever be over. First, the alimony must stop, and because I signed all the papers without reading them, because she had stated to the Policemen that she struck the first blow by digging her fingernails into my arm, and beating me on the chest. This is stated in the police report. I did not file against her, I just wanted it over. Never once did my attorney tell me that she could use this report against me, since she was the guilty party. I did not know anything about counter filing, nor was I told by my lawyer that was what I should do. I

hired a lawyer that was supposed to REPRESENT me, but not one time did he tell me to counter file against her, and that would stop the forthcoming alimony and court proceedings. She took her attack on me and turned it around that I had done this to her. It is still unbelievable to me that in America, someone could twist the law around when they had on file written statements that SHE ABUSED ME. I was defending myself. What has happened that we no longer have the right to defend ourselves in a court of law? What has happened that we pay a lawyer, one who is supposed to know the law, and he does not defend us, but instead drags the divorce out, and I was homeless during this time, as she had me removed from my home. I could not think, but this is what I paid the lawyer to do, DEFEND ME. Because he did not tell me to press charges against her, I have been sentenced to a divorce that will never end by having to send her monthly alimony and by her lawyer and mine dragging the court out to make it a ten year marriage qualifying her to draw from my Social Security. Even though it doesn't affect what I draw, she was never entitled to this. Once she started drawing my Social Security instead of her own and her husband's Railroad Benefits, the $500 alimony should have been stopped. I was under the impression that the alimony was only temporary. Only recently have I read all the hundreds of papers. I am expecting God to intercede and bring JUSTICE TO ME.

15. MIRACLE - There is one very 'SPECIAL' miracle that has taken place in my life. Last June 2007, this tall dark haired widow from Texas walked into the Senior Center in Douglasville, Georgia to learn to play Euchre, and I was sitting at the back of the room. A lady that she had met the day before, Fannie, took her around introducing her. I was seated, and when I looked into those beautiful blue eyes, my heart skipped a beat, and I knew that somehow she was to be the one for me. As she

looked at me, a twinkle came into her eyes, and the blue eyes began to dance, and I know we both loved each other at that moment. We fell in love and became two of the lucky ones to find love again. The roads we have traveled make us know that everyday together is a gift from God.

She had lost her husband to cancer after a fight of four and half years. She told me later that it was as if she had been in a great battle, and at the end, she lost the war. I think she had been pretty well off, but the years of fighting the cancer took a great tole on her, her pocketbook, and ate her very soul. She told me she did everything possible to keep him alive, both medically and spiritual. She had called the elders of the church, had them pray, and put it over the internet, and hundreds of prayers went up for him and his cure. She took him twice and had him anointed with oil. He would get better and then the cancer would pop up somewhere else. She watched him waste away to skin and bones, and took care of him herself, as she said that's what she wanted to do and what he wanted her to do, never leaving his side. She said she would take him from room to room in the wheel chair and tie him in, so he would not fall out, for he could somehow get the strength at the end to get himself out of bed, but could not stand on his feet and she would find him in the floor calling for her. The last ten nights she had him home, she slept with her body across the bottom part of his torso, so that he would have to reach for her neck, and this would wake her, and she would put her arms around his waist and pull him to his feet, and she said that he would be happy for a little while. His hands had swollen over twice their size, and she put him back in the hospital on Saturday afternoon. His body was already shutting down, and he was not getting any blood and oxygen to his feet, legs, arms and hands. On Monday morning, she had him moved to Hospice of East Texas in Tyler , Texas, by ambulance. Once the doctor examined him, she told Melba that he could not possibly live though the next day, and that she had to give him permission to die. This was something Melba said she felt she could not do, but the doctor told her she must, as he was holding on because of her, and that they had given him enough morphine that he would rest through the night, but when he awoke in the morning, she must tell him that it was alright for him to go. She was sitting beside his bed, holding his hand when he awoke, barely opening his eyes, and as he tried to speak, he could not. She said, "I read his lips, and he said, "I love you". She said, "I love you too, and I thank you for the wonderful life you have shared with me, but it is alright for you to go on...Besides, Marianna is waiting to meet her grandson." She said that he tried to smile, and gave it his best shot with a twinkle in his eye that told her that Marianna was already there to get him." Then he closed his eyes, and one hour and forty minutes later, the oxygen bag began to deflate, and when it got to his mouth, he was gone. No gasping for breath, an easy death compared to the last four years of his life. Mariana was his grandmother who died in Poland in 1948 after the war, but prior to the war, her son had come to America, and John's mother was already married, so when John was born, he was given to a family that took him from Philadelphia to Connecticut and raised him. His biological father, Marianna's son, died in 1939 with TB, and the letters to America stopped. Through the internet, Melba was able to find a man in Poland who helped her to find his family, even though they were all dead except from his Mother's family who was Catholic and went back to her husband after the birth of John. She had died, and an older brother, but they did not want to see him. His sister, a nun, made the remark to him when he called that his mother referred to him as her "love child", and she was bitter, and the nun hated John because of her mother's love for this lost child that financially she could not keep or raise. His father could not because he had TB and was dying. After staying put for two years, Melba left Texas and came to Douglasville, Georgia to try to start a new life, and called the Chamber of Commerce to see where Senior's met. She had a son living in Douglasville, and I had a daughter, so YES, THIS WAS A MIRACLE that GOD would help two lost lonely souls to find each other, to give us love again in the winter of our lives.

She told me that when someone you love so much, such as my Helen and her John that there is a part of that life that goes to memory, but another part, the living part of love must be passed to another human being, the hugging, the holding. Without it, life cannot began again, and the will to live just isn't there. Everyday, is a nothing day. I know that I was an easy prey for Mabel, for I was starved after nine months for that holding and hugging, and I thought she cared, but she had not lost a spouse to death, only to divorce, and both of her spouses were still living, so she did not have the slightest idea to what it is like to have them die, for as long as they are living, there is always a chance that, perhaps, sometime, the two will get back together again, but DEATH is final.

In a little book that Melba gave me, in the back, it says:

I am standing upon the seashore. A ship at my side spreads her white sails to the morning breeze and starts for the blue ocean. She is an object of beauty and strength. I stand and watch her until at length she hangs like a speck of white cloud just where the sea and sky come to mingle with each other.

Then someone at my side says "There she is gone!"

Gone Where?

Gone from sight. That is all. She is just as large in mast and hull and spar as she was when she left my side and she is just as able to bear her load of living freight to her destined port.

Her diminished size is in me, not in her, And just at the moment when someone at my side says "There she is gone!" there are other eyes watching her coming, and other voices ready to take up the glad shout "Here she comes!"

I know when Helen died that my grandson, John David, and my great grandson, David, were two of those shouting,

"HERE SHE COMES!"

And that is dying.

16. MIRACLE? I remember, well, the day when 18 B-17's left England in formation for our target for the day, and only eight returned. All around us, these beautiful B-17's and their crews being blown to bits, and others parachuting from the planes that had been hit crashing to the ground. I don't know if those men lived to hit the ground, was taken prison for the duration of the war, or if they were shot as they hit the ground or even shot later. I only know that is was a very sad day for all of us. The eight that returned were badly shot with holes in their planes, and many had been shot in their planes, so I will never know in this world just how many ten man crews in each of the ten lost planes actually survived. I don' t even know how many in the eight that returned that was alive and lived. I only know that our barracks became very empty, as many of them shared our barracks. I also know it was a miracle that our plane and crew returned without any of us being killed.

17. MIRACLE? Melba and I have talked at great length about which is easier, instant death, or weeks and months of slowly dying. Dying instantly gives a tremendous shock to the family, but to watch someone you love slowly die over a period of months, and climb to the top of the mountain one day, only to be slammed to the bottom of the ravine against the rocks.

It takes your money, takes your own health besides the tremendous cost, leaving the other spouse without any money to live on. In April of 1964, Melba's sister and her three children were killed in an automobile wreck. She was the oldest daughter, and Melba says that her father never got over the death of his oldest child, or the loss of three grandchildren. About twenty years later, her oldest brother's only daughter was killed in another automobile wreck, leaving two little girls. She was divorced, and her father and mother raised the two little girls, two and three years of age. Both are now nurses, and have their own families.

I know there is a GREATER POWER and someday, we shall meet the God who made us in His image face to face. Whatever wrongs, we have done in this life in which we have not made retribution or asked for forgiveness from that person, will escort us to that FINAL DESTINATION.

SO, I leave you with this thought *WHAT WILL YOU DO WITH THE MAN CALLED CHRIST? WILL YOU DIE WITH SINS THAT YOU HAVE NOT BEEN FORGIVEN FOR, AND TRIED TO SET RIGHT THE WRONGS THAT YOU HAVE DONE TO OTHERS? THERE WILL BE NO HIDING FROM JESUS ON THAT DAY. HE GAVE HIS LIFE FOR US. HE SAID TO TURN THE OTHER CHEEK AND TO PRAY FOR THOSE WHO SPITEFULLY USE YOU. I HAVE TRIED TO DO THIS, SINCE JUSTICE AND BEING FREE FROM THIS WOMAN NAMED MABEL, IS SOMETHING SHE CAN ONLY UNDO. WILL SHE? I DOUBT IT! THE BIBLE ALSO TALKS OF THE LOVE OF MONEY BEING THE ROOT OF ALL EVIL..........JUST AS THE RICH MAN TURNED AWAY SORRY WHEN CHRIST TOLD HIM TO GO AND GIVE HIS MONEY TO THE POOR. MABEL WILL FACE CHRIST SOMEDAY, AND PERHAPS, HE WILL ASK*

HER, "WHY DID YOU HIDE YOUR FACE FROM GENE AND YOURSELF ALL DURING THE COURT PROCEEDING CLAIMING YOU WERE AFRAID OF HIM." CHRIST KNOWS AND SHE KNOWS THAT IS A LIE. SHE MAY NOT HAVE TO FACE ME, BUT SHE WILL FACE GOD FOR HER LIES AND DECEIT AND USING AMERICA'S JUDICIAL SYSTEM TO STEAL FROM A MAN THAT LOVED HER FOR AWHILE.

TODAY, SHE DRAWS $500.00 PER MONTH ALIMONY FROM ME, SOCIAL SECURITY FROM ME (The Social Security office will not tell me how much she is getting since the divorce was final), and her ex husband, named Estes, who retired from the railroad has died, and she is drawing benefits from him. NOT BAD, for a woman that I met and married after my wife of fifty years died, that was living in a government subsidized apartment for $95 a month and claimed to have no money. She certainly made me believe that she loved me, and so I moved from the home Helen and I shared, and moved to Florida, where she had a daughter and also where it was an alimony state. Because I trusted her, my lawyer, and the judicial system of MY BEAUTIFUL AMERICA, I will be punished for this trust by having to pay her $500 a month for as long as one of us is living.. no one bothered to read the report that the policeman filed stating SHE HAD STRUCK THE FIRST BLOW, nor would they listen or even read a letter that I had prepared in my own self defense.

Also, there are original photos taken of me throughout my service career, and the other eight men who were with me during the missions over Germany, and enemy occupied France, Belgium and Holland.

I wish my old crew were here today to read this book, for I know that I have been blessed to have known GREAT MEN and WOMEN, with great strength and character to do what they had to do and survived a WORLD WAR.

CONSTITUTION OF THE UNITED STATES OF AMERICA HAVE YOU FORGOTTEN THIS CONSTITUTION? PLEASE DON'T, FOR MEN AND WOMEN HAVE FOUGHT AND DIED FOR THESE LIBERTIES - YOURS AND MINE. PLEASE DO NOT ABUSE THEM, FOR THIS WAS WRITTEN BY MEN OF GREAT COURAGE, CHARACTER AND GREAT MORAL FIBER. THIS IS WHAT HEAVEN WILL BE FILLED WITH, PEOPLE WHO LOVE OTHERS AS THEMSELVES. NOT FILLED WITH GREED, DECEIT, LUST AND LIES.......YOU WILL FIND THOSE PEOPLE IN HELL.

So much has happened since Mabel had me removed from our home, and I became AN AMERICAN HOMELESS VETERAN. How could this have happened? As I think back about the situation a few years ago, I realize how wrong I was the day when the officer asked me if I wanted to press charges against Mabel. Had I only known the way things were going to change my life, I would have taken the initiative and signed a warrant at that time, but I didn't realize how cold hearted she was and the fact that I would have to improve her financially.

I would not want the reader led to believe that this is my opinion of all women, because I know that there are still a lot of good loving and caring ladies in this world that appreciate having honorable and faithful husbands.

Yesterday, Melba and I went to Bay Pine Hospital to the pharmacy, as a new prescription that we had already paid for once was running out, and I had not heard anything from the pharmacy since receiving a letter stating that they only carried the generic, and could I take that. When I received the letter, Melba said that we needed to go down to the Sarasota

VA Clinic, and we did. The nurse said that I would have to get another prescription for the generic from the doctor not associated with the VA that had been called in when the VA sent me to the emergency room at Doctor's hospital to try to find out where my loss of blood was happening and to receive 4 pints of blood. Thankfully, the pharmacy was able to fill it, as they are very efficient. I will say that the woman at the VA clinic in Sarasota, had I listened to her, I would not have been able to get the medicine and would have had to put out another $250.00 to get it from a local pharmacy. As I had done that once already, and also had to put out almost $70.00 for a combination of three compounds to be mixed after they did the day procedure at Sarasota hospital burning out my Barrett's, I really did not have the money to do this. We had several extra expenditures, besides Christmas just passing and our trip back up to Douglasville, Georgia to be with our family. Anyway, for once, we felt the day had been successful.

Our new life together in Sunny Sarasota, Florida

MELBA

How beautiful life has become! I know now that I should have married a widow after Helen died, not a twice divorced woman. Melba, being a widow had her life dashed among the rocks and broken into a million pieces as did I. By walking that path, can one really understand the loneliness that overtakes our lives. There isn't anything worse than being alone and old, knowing that you have reached the winter of your life, and your spouse has died, and everyone goes home, and the house is empty, and you are left with memories. Memories that over power you. Everywhere I looked, there were memories of Helen. Many days, I would not open the blinds or answer the door. I would leave the car in the garage, and sit, and when I did get out, it was to go to the cemetery to sit at her grave and ask, "Why didn't you take me too, or take me instead?" The will to live was lost, and I did not think that I would ever find this feeling again.

Please do not confuse Mabel, my 2nd wife with MELBA, my present wife, for there are worlds of difference between these two women. Mabel did not like hugging and slept with her back to me. She became a very cold fish. From the time of my two brain surgeries in 1999, she was no longer a wife to me.

Melba is right the opposite. From the first night, she asked if I wanted to spend the night with her, we slept in the raw and held each other tight. We have slept in each others arms since that night. I know only too well what it is like for two people to become one, as God intended. It is like neither of us can get enough of the touching, holding, loving that now fills both our lives, and I know this woman loves me with all her heart, and she knows that I feel the same way. God brought us together at the Senior place in Douglasville, Georgia, and our friends that we played cards with watched as the instant love flourished like flower blossoms from the rain and sunshine, growing more beautiful every day. I never want to be alone again, but then neither of us wanted to be alone. We did not choose that our spouses of many years would die. Now, I know that God did really save the best for last. For the first time in many years, I am content, totally comfortable and totally at ease. I look at her, and I see in her eyes a love for me that I had long forgot could exist between two human beings. I thank God everyday for bringing her into my life.

Sometimes, I cannot believe that I was 83 in September, five days after we married, and she will be seventy June 22nd.

We both have began to gain back the lost weight, for one of us cooks everyday. It is so easy loving her. Just as she says, "Loving me is easier than anything she has ever done before."

We like doing the same things music, cooking, keeping our place clean, and we do it as a team, so it isn't work when one does for the other out of love.

In the early morning hours, we hold each other close and make beautiful music together. Thank you, God, for such a wonderful love to fill my life. I know that I never want to be without her. I also know she wants to be with me, and that is what makes life so very good again. We share everything, our dreams, our thoughts, our life, everything. I know if she had a magic wand, she would wipe away the bad times with Mabel, but there are no magic wands, and so we can only pray that God will lead us to someone who can find the way through this tangled Florida law that holds me prisoner to a woman whom I barely knew, and she had three children by another man, this man called Estes. Everything Helen and I worked for, this woman took, the money from our home in Danville, all the furniture, household goods. The money from the sale of the doublewide here in Sarasota that was sold. She got the money and everything, and I got the SHAFT! I just wish it would stop now. It is time for her to get on with her life and get the HELL out of mine. I don't know why I should have to give until I bleed, and have to tell her where I live, when I marry, and everything about my life. I know nothing about hers. It is so hard to believe that I fought for this country, got shot at constantly over Germany, and risked my life, so that a divorced woman could screw my life up so much and still control a portion of it. If I could, I'd pay her off, but she got the money from the sale of the house. I had two boxes with my service records and medals, and a few clothes. I did not even get all my clothing, and I got nothing that belonged to Helen and me. She took that too.

I love Melba, and we have the right to the pursuit of happiness under the bill of rights. Has our country gotten so bad, that we are enslaved in certain states by judicial systems that seek revenge rather than justice?.

In spite of everything, Melba and I wake up, loving each other, holding each other, and enjoying just being together. I wouldn't want to live if I didn't have her, and I know she feels the same way. When we leave this world to our heavenly home, we both pray that God will take us together, for neither of us want to walk down that lonesome road again. WE HAVE FOUND EACH OTHER WITH THE GRACE OF GOD, AND WE KNOW WE ARE AMONG THE LUCKY ONES.

The doublewide that we purchased is in a senior park, and they keep the grass mowed, as neither of us are really up to keeping up a large place, and it is just right for us. Sometimes, we get homesick for Douglasville and think we may move back there, but we both know we just need to visit occasionally and see our family and friends and then return to Florida, where the doctors that we both know and trust live. The medical facilities here are very good, and many doctors from all over the world are here. Twice, I know that by moving here, my life was saved, both with the two brain surgeries and then when Melba and I moved here to find that I was short a half gallon of blood. To know that good health care is here and it is warm in the winter keeps us here.

We know that once we get some of the unpleasant tasks put aside that we will be free to go to the senior center here and make new friends here in the park and other places.

Whatever God has in store for us, we will meet the challenges together. We love each other, a gift from God, and that is all that really matters.

We both remember our wedding vows TO HAVE AND TO HOLD FROM THIS DAY FORWARD.

I know if everyone could find what we feel for each other that our God has been so good to bring into our lives that there would be no fighting, fussing, divorces, for there would only be time to do what the Good Book says, "Forsaking all others". Putting our own house in order FIRST.

Melba took me to Texas to meet her five brothers and another son and his family. She wanted them to meet and love me as she does. She also took me to see certain friends that were special to her. It was an enjoyable trip.

She also took me to Pt St Lucie to meet her only living aunt, her son, daughter-in-law, and two granddaughters, and also another first cousin that she has that lives there.

She has a nice family, and I am proud to be a part of them, just as she is proud of my family.

I still have not met her youngest granddaughter and youngest grandson who live in Arizona and the state of Washington. Perhaps, when summer or spring comes, we can meet them at their fathers in Georgia.

We went to see my only living sister, Merle, before Thanksgiving, and she is in a nursing home in League City, Texas. Neither of us would not take for the look on her face when I walked in. If it were not for this alimony, I would have more money to go to see her, and my own family. I guess I am just tired of having someone who treated me so shabby fly around the country on my retirement money, my Social Security and whatever else she has got from me. I would not have her back for all the money in the world, and I cannot ever stop loving my beautiful Yellow Rose of Texas that God picked for me and transplanted in Georgia, so that I could pick this beautiful Rose to have for my own.

I guess more than anything, I hope this book will accomplish awareness for our young and old. Hopefully, it will help them to realize that anything worth having is worth fighting for, and that America is only as good as her people.

With people from all over the world in Sarasota, Florida, sometimes, I hate the congestion that all the snowbirds and foreigners create here this time of year. Everywhere we go, it is mobs of people. The highways and streets are filled with people who drive like maniacs. There are many good people who come here, but many are very rude from different parts of our own United States. Perhaps, it is the way they live in their little neck of the world.

It is every person's obligation to make a living for themselves, to be responsible for themselves. I hope all of you will remember that it is not someone else's responsibility to take care of you, for THAT IS YOUR JOB. When you take from someone else, you will pay, either with your soul in the next world, or right here on earth.

I was lucky to have a daughter that loved me, and I could go there and stay with her and her husband for seven months to get on my feet and save enough money to rent a small cheap apartment and buy used furniture from some of her friends that had lost their parents, and what else, I needed in the way of furnishing, she loaned me a loveseat, a dining table, and I bought a TV and dishes, towels and other household needs.

Take care of yourselves first, for without your own health, you cannot help yourself or others.

May God Bless You All, and LONG LIVE AMERICA, THE BEAUTIFUL.

Our Wedding Party: Sheila Gold, Gina and Mark Mallory, Joyce Cooper, Dusty Cantrell, Melba and Gene Browning, Maggie Gold, Sarah Mallory holding Bella Gold, Josh Price and Jake Mallory

Final Thoughts

This is another one of those sleepless nights. I think perhaps all older people go through them. Times, when we can sleep like a baby, and then other times, when we cannot sleep at all. So many things running through my mind now, as I sit here and think about the past, the present and the future.

I remember on one of our missions, when one of the planes in our formation was hit with flak. Instead of bursting into flames, or nose diving, it went into a spirror going down. Sitting in the ball turret hanging out of the bottom of our B-17, I had a perfect view. As the plane went down, with each circle, a man would jump, and the parachute would open, and down he would go. I watched this until the one jumped, his parachute was not hooked to his harness, and as he jumped from the plane, he was trying to hook it to the harness, but the wind was much too strong, and I watched as the parachute flew away from him, and he tumbled toward the ground with nothing to stop the fall.

I don't know if he was the ball turret gunner, for we could not wear a parachute, only our harness, as there was not enough room in the turret to wear a parachute, but it was just inside the plane, so we could grab it and hook it, should we need it. Our radio operator always had mine handy for me, and always said

123

that he would not leave the plane without me. I watched as the man flew into space tumbling toward the ground. I will never forget that as long as I live. Even yesterday, I thought about it and could still see him, knowing in my heart that when he hit the ground, if he made it, he would slam to his death.

I know why so many Veterans cannot talk about the war. There are so many things that happened that are too terrible for our minds to go back there. The ones lucky enough to come home, wanted to try to put those visions they had seen out of their minds forever, and try in the only way they could to get on with their lives. Some were able; some became alcoholics, drug users, many things to try to blot out the nightmares that roamed through their minds. Visions of their best buddies being blown to bits beside them, with their blood and guts scattered all over them. War is truly HELL.

Somehow, I wish that all the world could find peace. Greed and the love of money and power seem to drive some to the brink, such as Hitler. Then there are those who are so hyped up that they will believe and follow anyone, even to death. Too many will not sit down and listen to reason. It appears to be all about ME, anymore, and was true though out the birth of our world.

When Jesus walked this earth, He tried to teach us love and mercy, and look what they did to him. An innocent man, like so many since, persecuted for something they did not do. Hatred seems to run rampid. There are those who will pretend to be our friends or to love us, and then when they get a chance to take one for everything they have, they turn their back on you and care not if you have a crust of bread, a shirt on your back. I know now that Mabel Holycross, my second wife, was that way. I really thought she loved me, but it was a front to get what I worked for and what my wife Helen that died worked for, and once she managed to do this, she was finished with me. I was someone to get her a paycheck coming in, someone to steal from. All in the name of love, and because of my loneliness, I was taken in by what I thought was a woman who loved me. I know that I could not have been so very wrong. I knew that she had no money, and I tried to be fair with her, and never, did I want to put anyone in jail, much less a woman. Being naive and trusting, got me where I am today, her prisoner until the day one of us dies. What I hate the worse, is getting Melba involved in a situation in which she had nothing to do with, and has helped me with everything she has, love, money, caring. I am happy that I found her and that God brought her into my life. So many will not stop to help the homeless, or someone sick, as we don't want to get involved. Then we are bombarded with the phony ministers on television begging for money. You look at them and see the plush golden drapes, beautiful furniture and the way they are dressed in the finest, and I wonder why they do not sell their own belongings and live in much smaller homes and give THEIR money to the poor, the starving. None of us need the giant homes, we just need a place to lay our heads at night, a little food and someone to love that loves us in return. That is the greatest gift we can have.

We have those in power who fight for money and power. Not realizing that money and power change hands. John Ringling, of the Ringling circus is a good example of that. He came here with enormous wealth, and built the very finist in Sarasota, but at the end he died with nothing. He lost the love of his life in her fifty's, and the money in the world could not save her. He later married again, but it was not a good marriage. He did so much for Sarasota, only to be forgotten when he was broke and could no longer do anything to make it a great city. At one time, he had, "The Greatest Show On Earth." A life of glitz and glamour. This beautiful paradise where he came and built so much became ruins, and was finally taken over by the state of Florida and the City of Sarasota. It is a beautiful place once again, with so much history. He died in Chicago a broken man both financially and spiritually.

I think about my own biological mother, who did not want me or her other four children, one dying young. She gave all of us up without a fight, and lived in the same town where we lived, married another man, and raised HIS children. Never once sending a birthday card, Christmas card or acknowledging us in anyway. Our mother became Florence Nelson who married my father a few years after the divorce. I know my father had a hard time trying to raise four children, but he managed, and all did well, except for my sister who was murdered by a jealous husband whom she was trying to divorce.

NO one person owns another. We are all God's children, and we belong to HIM. Our wives, children, friends, those we love actually belong to God, and at anytime He can take them back to himself, trying to teach us that We ALL BELONG TO GOD, and that our family and friends are given to us to bring us joy and happiness for a short time on earth. We never know how short that time is going to be.

The greatest gift we can ever receive or give is LOVE, for it is our greatest gift from our FATHER above.

I remember Sheila telling me the last thing that her son, John David, read to her was:

FOOTPRINTS

One night a man had a dream. He dreamed he was walking along the beach with the LORD. Across the sky flashed scenes from his life. For each scene, he noticed two sets of footprints, in the sand. One belonged to him, and the other the LORD.

When the last scene of his life flashed before him, he looked back at the footprints in the sand. He noticed that many times along the path of his life. there was only one set of prints. He also noticed that it happened at the very lowest and saddest times in his life.

This really bothered him, and he questioned the LORD about. "LORD, you said that once I decided to follow you, you'd walk with me, all the way. But I have noticed that during the most troublesome things in my life, there is only one set of footprints. I don't understand why when I needed you the most you would leave me."

The LORD replied, "My precious, precious child, I love you, and I would never leave you. During your times of trial and suffering, when you see only one set of footprints, it was then that I carried you."

Perhaps, John David, felt that would be the last time he would see his mother in this life and was trying to prepare her for something about to happen, which I am sure he did not know what. Somehow, I feel the message that he left to her was "Mom, in the days ahead, when I will be taken to another world, remember that when you are unable to walk and times are so sad and hard for you, that those will be the times when the LORD will carry you across the sand until you can stand alone on your own again."

My wife, Melba, tells me that when her sister and her three children were killed in a car wreck, and she lived next door to them, that she felt they had to move because of too many memories. Then she says, "I try to forget the loneliness and remember that they all belonged to the LORD, and that HE only loaned them to us to brighten up our lives for awhile, and I feel that HE allowed an angel, my sister, to walk with us for awhile, and for that I will forever be grateful." We all know what is said, "That it is better to have loved and lost than never to have loved at all." I know that we never forget these people, they live in our hearts forever, but we can be happy that we know they were good and awaiting us for when it becomes our turn to enter the gates of Heaven, and they will be sitting on the far side banks of Jordan waiting to say, "HERE he or she comes!" While hearts on this side are sad, hearts on that side, will be happy.

Let us try not to be selfish and hurt others, but pray for those who spitefully use us, who have stolen things that do not belong to them, who have lied about us in order to get what they wanted with no thought of tomorrow, and their day when they come FACE TO FACE with our SAVIOR. I just want him to say, "Welcome home, and well done my child."

I believe that WORLD WAR I and WORLD WAR II, were different from the wars today that they call police action. We knew what we were fighting for..........FREEDOM. Today, it is different, our young people go to war for economic reasons, such as oil, greed of men, and if only these men could realize that someday, their wealth will vanish, and their greedy war would have been in vain. It isn't likely that their future generations will even have a decent world to live in, much less all the money their forefathers have lied and stole to achieve.

There have always been wars, and I believe that God expects us to stand up and fight for what belongs to us or to help others, but the money is only good if it is used to help others in need. All of us have a job to do on this earth, and the bible plainly tells us if man does not work, he shall not eat. Sometimes, a person needs a helping hand, but they do not need to be on welfare for all their lives and have other generations on welfare. After all, every cent we have actually belongs to God. He has simply made us the custodian over a certain amount to see if we will use it for the good.

So many try to justify their actions. There is a small still voice that lives inside us, and we must all learn to listen to that little voice, for it will guide us, if we will let it. Wrong cannot be justified, never. If you have wronged another, then you are to try to right that wrong.

Our country should never have done away with the draft, for this makes us vulnerable to being over taken. Every young adult should have to give two years in the service of his country. Not just fighting, but to repair the infrastructure of our land, building parks, restoring our history, building community centers, teaching the youth in summer camps, or how to make it, should the electricity go out or if they have to go out and find their dinner in the woods and fields, and how to cook what they have found.

If this book has helped one person to change their lives from bad to finding the good in all of us and working toward all brotherhood, then I have fulfilled my job.

I know only too well that all the real HEROS are those that never came home, and their wives and families that had to go on with life without them. Thousands and thousands of young women became widows and children became fatherless. How can I express to all those families how sorry I am. I will always remember all of those in my prayers, and I know now that many of those women and children have also passed to the other world and are at peace now.

May God bless all of you that worked so hard all over the world to see that your men could fight and defend all of you.

For the many wonderful soldiers that I have met all over the world and at the American Legion in Douglasville, Georgia, and for all the men at Martins and the Seniors at the Senior Center, and all of my friends that I worked with through the years, and all the many others too numerous to name, your memories live in my heart, and

I AM PROUD TO BE AN AMERICAN AND PROUD OF MY FAMILY AND FRIENDS.

MAY GOD BLESS AND KEEP YOU, AND MAY YOU ALWAYS KNOW THAT AMERICA IS THE GREATEST COUNTRY ON EARTH.

For your love and understanding to stand behind those you loved and those you lost, MAY GOD FOREVER LIVE IN YOUR HEARTS, for someday, we SHALL all meet again.

MY DREAM

Last night, Wednesday, April 3, 2008, I had this crazy dream. I do not know if it was because Melba had been working on the book, copying it to present to a publisher, and my old crew was on my mind.

I dreamed that we had flown another mission and got back to England, but the pilot, co-pilot, and bombardier had all been wounded, and I was in the hospital with the pilot and co-pilot. I got a phone call that said the bombardier was not expected to live, and the call was from Sheila, my daughter, who had not been born when we were in England on our missions. She was in Helen's stomach growing into a baby that was born Thanksgiving day after my return to America. This David L. Taylor, was the one who refused to fly anymore missions after the flight where the oxygen tank had been hit by flak up in the nose of the plane, and it flew around and caused confusion for the navigator and the bombardier. I came up out of the ball turret at that time to help the bombardier as when he pushed the toggle switch and said, "Bombs Away", the bombs did not fall, and David needed help on the other end to get them to fall. David was almost blown out of the plane, and Don, the top turret gunner, kept him from falling out through the bomb-bay, so perhaps, his reason for never flying again was

130

a feeling of predestination that he would be killed. One never knows why a member of the crew looses their courage, but as I said before, "It could have happened to any of us."

David was on a different floor from the pilot and co-pilot in my dream, so at that time, I asked Don how we got the plane back to England, and he said, "Don't you remember, I called you to fly co-pilot, and I flew the plane back and landed." Before I went and checked on David Taylor, I woke up from my dream. All the details of the dream were so vivid that I have been unable to get it off my mind.

This morning, I called my daughter, Sheila, who lives in Georgia, to see if she would check Logan. West Virginia and see if she could find a David Taylor living there. I called a Debra Taylor who was Debra Brown, and I have not heard back from her, so do not know if her husband is related to David or not.

We had gone to see David once after the war and he and his brother owned a furniture store, called Taylor's Furniture in Logan, West Virginia.

The young lady that answered the phone said there wasn't a furniture store named Taylor's Furniture anymore, but then that was a long time ago. Debra Taylor called me back and said that her husband did not know this David Taylor, and that he no longer lived in Logan, West Virginia, so I do not know if he has died or not. I only know that Charles McFall and I, are still living out of the original ten man crew.

Perhaps, David Taylor died and is buried at Logan, West Virginia, or in a Veteran's cemetery, for in later years, I know that he was trying to get his service record corrected, and I hope that he was successful.

Melba's father volunteered and had five children. He said one night the government came into their barracks and got all of the men and took them and put them on planes. He was a foot soldier. Once they were in the planes, the man in charge said, "You are now paratroopers." They had no training to be a paratrooper. He said they flew them to Siapan, and opened the door and pushed them out one at a time, and he was told to jump, and he said, "I'm not jumping," but he said, "He was bigger than me," and he said, "Oh, yes, you are," and he gave him a push out of the plane. Of course, the parachutes opened as they were pushed from the planes, for being hooked to the line and jumping pulled the rip cord to open the chute. Once he landed on the ground, he became a foot soldier again. Every serviceman has a story to tell. Just as every person on earth has a story to tell, for all of our lives are different, and so many lessons are to be learned in this life.

We can all rest assured that we are not getting out of this life alive. I just want to be taken up when my time comes. I am in no hurry, as I love my wife and life. I am thankful for such a beautiful world filled with people who love me and I can love in return. I know that my Melba brought me back to life. She gave me a reason to live again. Thank you, Darling!

I remember when Dick Van Dyke and his young bride Marge were preparing to head for California. They stopped in at Barkman Chevrolet garage where Bill Willeck was shop foreman and I was doing body work at the time. Bill gave him his 1941 Chevrolet to take to California. Dick was driving a Ford at that time, and had a trailer hitch that he hooked the Chevrolet to, and I wonder if he remembers this. They started out and got somewhere in the center of Missouri when the Ford broke down, they transferred the trailer hitch to the back of the Chevy and pulled the Ford on to California. I am sure they had a rough time for awhile until he finally made it big in the movie industry. Marge's mother was married to Bill Willeck, and they later went to visit them at Dick's ranch in Arizona.

Bill would often talk about the times that they went to visit them on Dick and Marge's ranch where he and Mamie would sleep in the guest house. While they visited with their daughter and son-in-law, this was where they stayed, in the guest house. I remember Dick and Jerry starting out doing pantomime to entertain the locals of Danville, Illinois. Before his journey to California, he was in several presentations on the stage of Kathryn Randolph's theater, know as the Red Mask Theater of Danville. His father was known as Cookie Van Dyke in the Danville area. Later, the well known Gene Hackman, was active in the Red Mask Theater also. I remember all this before I was involved with Red Mask, and I feel real honored to have known these people.

There are so very many memories that flood my mind as I try to remember things that would interest you as you read about my life.

I also remember dining at Connor's restaurant who was an uncle to Donald O'Connor. I never really met Donald, but I always managed to watch the movies in which he appeared. Knowing that his roots had been deeply planted in the Danville, Illinois area. These are some of my pleasant memories.

Bobby Short, I never met, because he was before my time. I realize that he had gone on to become a household word.

I am proud to have come from the same area as these well known people.

I also know that to have been married to Helen for a little over fifty years was also a milestone in my life.

I know that I had to go through the divorce from MABEL, as that is the only way that I could have met this wonderful lady from Texas, who is now the love of my life, and my wife, MELBA JOYCE ARCHER BROWNING, so just how LUCKY can a guy be? She went through her hardship when her husband died. She was a widow, and I believe that when a person has lost their spouse to death, then they need to marry someone who has also lost their spouse to death, for this is the ONLY way the other can really understand.

One time, my daughter, Sheila, told me about one of Mike's aunt's coming to Virginia to a funeral. Sheila said, "She was a wailer." I said, "You mean that she goes out and catches whales?" Sheila laughed and said, "No, Dad, I mean she really cried hard at the funeral, so I referred to her as a wailer."

We are happy and God has blessed us so much to have found love again in the WINTER OF OUR LIVES.

Printed in the United States
137079LV00004B/3/P